Grains of Sand

TALES OF A PARANORMAL LIFE

BRIAN J. CANO

Roswell Press

Mechanicsburg, Pennsylvania

an imprint of Sunbury Press, Inc.
Mechanicsburg, PA USA

FIRST ROSWELL PRESS EDITION: February 2022

Set in Garamond. Interior design by Chris Fenwick | Cover by Brian Cano | Edited by Chris Fenwick.

Publisher's Cataloging-in-Publication Data
Names: Cano, Brian J., author.
Title: Grains of Sand / Brian J. Cano.
Description: Revised trade paperback edition. | Mechanicsburg, Pennsylvania: Roswell Press, 2022.
Summary: One of today's most respected researchers invites readers on an intimate journey through some of his most memorable experiences and the existential lessons they hold for us all.
Identifiers: ISBN 978-1-62006-906-6 (softcover).
Subjects: BISAC: BIOGRAPHY & AUTOBIOGRAPHY / Personal Memoirs | BODY, MIND & SPIRIT / Unexplained Phenomena | BODY, MIND & SPIRIT / Supernatural

Continue the Enlightenment!

To my mother and father, who taught me to always believe in myself

and that anything is possible when you work hard to earn it.

Contents

Preface

I've been a paranormal investigator for almost twenty years, but only within that interval of time was the moniker given to a pursuit that has spanned my entire life—solving mysteries, discovering truths, excavating knowledge.

For years, I've dreamed of writing a book. Truth be told, I'd hoped to write a shelf's worth by this point in my life, but I cannot lament the events that have taken me on a tour of all that lies within these pages. One cannot write a survey of life without having lived some of it.

I also take full responsibility for erecting plenty of mental roadblocks along the way. I knew a book was in me, but I wrestled with the topic. In school, I wanted to write fiction, especially fantasy and sci-fi. I was great with beginnings and endings but completely lost when it came to middles. I also lacked the discipline to sit down and stick it out over the long haul. I'd get bored and abandon story ideas, never to revisit them. Then I found myself living a life full of fantastic true stories, but I struggled to recognize their value to others and therefore never thought of them as writing material.

Whenever I pondered writing a paranormal book, I tended to skew towards process and instruction—a manual or a guide to conducting investigations. But that plan never quite seemed to click. Plenty have gone before me and taken that route; many of their books sit on my shelf even now. What could I possibly add to the current collective knowledge base? I had to write something worth the effort, something that would be entertaining and yet educate on some level, but what would that be? What did I have to offer?

Then one day, I had the sad task of going through some old footage searching for a specific interview of my friend and mentor, Rosemary Ellen Guiley, who had recently passed away. Her advice, as well as the multitude of books she wrote about the paranormal, had taught me much. Finding the clip, I simply sat back and watched, taking in her words as if for the first time.

When asked about her feelings on the future and evolution of paranormal investigating, she said, "At some point, our technology may mature and change and develop to the point where we can reliably capture evidence of the unknown. I believe we have the best chance for this with our audio recording, that we may be able to develop voice devices that will deliver proof of the afterlife, but when that day will be at hand, nobody really knows."

What followed next struck a chord within me. Though I had heard it when I filmed the interview, and during subsequent viewings, it hadn't stirred me to action until now.

"In the meantime, investigators should record their subjective experiences along with the hard data. What we see, hear, feel, and experience through our own physical senses winds up making us really the best investigation instrument that we have out there—the human body."

My original takeaway had been that our bodies are the best pieces of equipment we can bring to any investigation, but now, something else stood out. Rosemary was saying that anecdotal evidence is important too; the telling of one's experiences is indeed valuable! So, what did I have to offer in a book? My experiences! The kind of life lessons that don't become apparent until time elapses and, upon reflection, the narrative completes itself. It seemed so simple, and yet I'd managed to overlook it for so long.

A question I get asked all the time is, "What experience changed you from a skeptic to a believer?" But I cannot point to only one. As I investigated the paranormal, I took each experience as I would a grain of sand. By itself, it didn't appear to be of much relevance. I'd look at it, then drop it to the floor. As time went on, however, I had more and more experiences, complete with the same discarding of the grains. Eventually, I looked down at my feet and saw that I was standing on a beach. It stretched to either side of me, far off into the horizon. A single grain of sand might seem inconsequential, but this was much greater. I was forced to reconsider what it all meant. Each grain of sand was a story at my feet. I only had to gather them up and begin writing. Thank you, Rosemary.

Essentially, it's Story Time with Brian, and as your humble narrator, I hope these tales of my evolution will help as you walk along your own beach. You have plenty of time to figure things out. Step one is to look down and simply notice.

Come, walk with me, won't you?

1

The Bad Touch

When speaking at events, I often ask the audience, "What is the most important piece of equipment to bring on any investigation?" I usually get varied responses, from audio equipment to EMF detectors and more. Eventually, we arrive at the desired answer: your body. I go on to say that yes, your body is the best piece of equipment—your five senses, nay, your six senses (as I place a finger upon my forehead), wait, your *seven* senses! That one throws everybody off for a second as I pause to let them ponder what it could be. What is our seventh sense? It's common sense, and it is definitely one we should employ more often.

Though I teach it today, it took a long time for me to accept that the body was a meter of paranormal activity. I'd heard it spoken, read about it once or twice, but not until many years after I'd had an experience of my own could I pass it on to others with conviction. Allow me to explain.

***

The year was 2005. Our local cable access show *Scared on Staten Island!* had been running for three years, and we'd exhausted local places to showcase. It was time to venture across our four bridges. One of the first places we chose to explore outside of Staten Island was Philadelphia. Namely, Eastern State Penitentiary. Many of you holding this book will immediately know the character and stories of that infamous prison, but at the time, our team only knew that it looked like a castle, and that alone had our imaginations running overtime. Eastern State Penitentiary had been an experiment in creating a system of incarceration that would rehabilitate prisoners and instill true penitence in them. Unlike today's jails, prisoners at Eastern State spent most of their time in solitary confinement; they rarely saw or were allowed to interact with other inmates. Guards' identities were obscured to protect them from possible retaliation on the outside. It was the penal equivalent of "Stand in the corner and think about what you've done!" As time went on, the rules changed and policies were modified, and Eastern State became more like other prisons. It had its share of escapes and escape attempts. There were a few inmates of note, like Willie Sutton and Al Capone. And it would be the biggest place we'd ever investigated.

We scouted in advance, took the guided tour. Then the time came to get our gear and get on the case. We were undertaking this investigation at a time when the paranormal field was still in its public infancy. Names like Holzer and Warren were only known by those within the mystical circles or old enough to have seen the news reports when they popped up. Two plumbers and their crew were the new kids on the block, and with their television show lighting up the airwaves, they opened up many doors for people to admit their belief in ghosts. It also gave us something to compare our show with. What influenced me most while watching *Ghost Hunters* (the afore mentioned plumbers) was the need for technical equipment. On this investigation to Eastern State Penitentiary, I would break out my first EMF detector—the E.L.F. Zone meter. I was so happy to be employing a technical device on our program. Looking back, I realize it was not the pinnacle of technology, but for a novice starting out, it was something, and we all have to start somewhere. I lovingly refer to it now as the Fisher Price–My First EMF Detector.

As we drove down the New Jersey Turnpike, the mood was one of excitement, pondering what awaited us in Philly. I was interested to see what more I would gather with the new equipment. Before then, we'd been primarily urban explorers. Sure, we looked around for ghosts, but our arsenal consisted of nothing more high-tech than some toy cars, ropes, and a bottle of baby powder. This time I had my new EMF detector and a digital audio recorder. I was ready to up my game. I had no clue that my best piece of equipment had been with me all along.

My memory of rolling into the prison feels like a music video. *The gates swing wide, and the van enters. Cut to a low-angle shot of the vehicle as the side door slides open. Boots hit the ground in slow motion. Medium shot: cases and cases of equipment are unloaded and hauled into the building. We all wear sunglasses. "Sabotage" by the Beastie Boys echoes through the courtyard from the restaurant across the street. The rock stars have arrived.* At least, that's how I fantasize about it in my mind. In reality, I imagine we were bickering or making silly jokes. Chris probably tripped over something, and Greg likely had to call home and check-in. We'd been friends for many years, so our personalities and peccadilloes were part of our standard operating procedure. Whatever the reality of our arrival was, I do remember the following events pretty clearly.

A few hours had passed as we set up to film our documentary. The tour guide had taken us around and shown us the hot spots, given us the basic rules, then left us to our own devices. We set up the stationary cameras, shot some B roll of the exterior, and even filmed a funny bit in the courtyard where we pretended to be criminals getting admitted into the prison for processing. (I shot that piece and was conveniently not one of the soon-to-be incarcerated!) Shortly after, we were ready to begin the investigation. It was then that I noticed something.

Unsure if it had come on gradually or all at once, I became aware of a pain in my body. It was of a personal nature—to be blunt, it was in my groin. It had become difficult to walk, impossible to stand, and generally uncomfortable no matter how I positioned myself. I tried to play it off and ignore it, but I could not do so for very long. As I hobbled about the cell blocks, Chris noticed and asked if I was okay.

"I don't know; this pain came out of nowhere," I replied.

"Perhaps you're getting your period."

Such was the humor between close friends in their twenties. The pain was dismissed, and any weakness was ripe for ridicule. But as I laughed it off, I tried to figure out the cause. Was it an early onset hernia? My back hadn't always been the greatest; perhaps groin discomfort was a symptom of some new era of spinal impropriety. Maybe during the load-out, I had lifted one of the heavy cases the wrong way. A bad twist or jerk could have upset my plumbing. If I gave it some rest, like a pulled muscle, it might return to normal on its own. Yes, a few moments of rest was what I needed.

"I'm going to go outside and get some air," I resolved.

I couldn't imagine enduring the entire night with this throbbing pain in my nether regions, so I prayed that the break would return me to normal. I crossed the street and sat on a bench next to the parking lot. As the sun set, painting the sky in a riot of reds, oranges, and pinks, I gazed upon the castle-like prison and let my mind wander to another time. As medieval musings washed over me, I began to feel better. Whatever had been affecting me must have been a random, passing pain. It was time to get back to work.

Re-entering the prison, I strode into the central hub where we'd set up our home base. The crew was eager to split up and explore the penitentiary, but as I grabbed a camera and my meter, the pain crept back. Like the growing prison shadows brought on by the departure of sunlight, my discomfort grew minute by minute until it was back in full force. I didn't know what to do. I started to panic as I considered the grander implications of what a pain like that could indicate.

"Okay, let's get going—Brian, you'll be heading to cell block one," Chris announced as he detailed the first-period assignments. Despite my agony, I thought it best to distract myself with the task at hand. I could book a doctor's appointment the next day when I got home. I'd worry about it then—for now, I just had to get through the night.

And so it went that evening. I struggled the entire time, but I made it. The paranormal details of that adventure were documented in *SCARED! Eastern State Penitentiary*. The night was filled with incidents and mysterious happenings. We experienced much and learned a few things as well. However, my most significant lesson would not be realized until many years later

***

2012. Philadelphia. I was back in town attending a paranormal event, and the evening's investigation would take place in none other than Eastern State Penitentiary. Seven years had passed since we filmed the documentary, and I endured that intense groin pain. I hadn't thought about it since because after I got home, the pain subsided. I never had it checked, and it never returned.

Since then, I had been back to Eastern State several times, but only as a tourist, never attempting to contact the Other Side during those visits. And with the passing of years, many things had changed. I had gone from a skeptic to a skeptical believer, having had many experiences I couldn't fully explain. *SCARED!* had evolved and grown, and we'd made many more documentaries, including a pivotal one at a place called The Grand Midway Hotel. I'd toured the country and spoken at paranormal conventions. I'd even ended up on the cast of *Haunted Collector* with John Zaffis, the opportunity that had landed me back at Eastern State as one of this evening's celebrity investigators.

I'd always considered events like this to be introductory for the attendees. In other words, one should not expect to experience anything profound due to all the people around. It's hard enough to recognize paranormal activity in a small group, much less with a large crowd. But I would soon be proven wrong.

Eastern State is laid out like a wagon wheel. At the center is a hub where the guards used to be stationed. Radiating out from that central point are the cell blocks, forming the spokes of the wheel. From their central vantage point, guards could have easily looked down any cell block and monitored what was going on. All event attendees were gathered in that hub, talking and socializing until we were broken up into groups. The celebrity investigators were assigned to individual cell blocks, and attendees would rotate through different cell blocks each period, so they could work with everyone and experience different ways of investigating. I was demonstrating my go-to techniques at that time: iPad apps and burst EVP sessions. Each period lasted about 45 minutes, and at the end of each period, everyone would return to the hub to briefly share their stories before moving on to the next area.

Shouted words echoed down the corridor: "Okay! Time to rotate!" As I walked back with my group, they marveled at the experience they'd just had and thanked me for giving them some things to think about. I nodded and smiled. My goal at such events was to get people to think differently. Not just emulate what they saw on television but also truly understand the concepts and be open to alternate explanations. The irony would become apparent in the moments that followed.

From floor to curved ceiling, the hub was a cacophony of laughter, elation, gasps, and hushed tones as excited attendees spun tales of unbelievable occurrences. A few of us professionals had gathered near a plexiglass case containing a model of the prison.

"How did it go?" Aaron asked.

"Not bad. Got a few bites, I think," I responded.

We compared notes briefly and discussed what was going on later that night. Just then, another pair of investigators, one donning a look of amused astonishment, walked over to the model.

"Chris, tell them what you just told me," Billy pushed.

Chris Fleming, psychic and paranormal investigator, looked at us and rolled his eyes. He then leaned in close and said in a low voice, "I got touched in the balls."

As the others snickered and began to joke, I cocked my head and thought to myself: *of course he did—for two reasons*. First, he was psychic. Such communication and happenings would be common to him. Second, he was in good physical shape, toned, and wearing a t-shirt that was perhaps a size too small on purpose. It was no surprise to me that in prison, he . . .

There it was—the moment of revelation. We were in a prison!

A light bulb had been turned on and was burning above my head, trying to access a long-forgotten memory. Images of that creepy shower scene from *The Shawshank Redemption* flooded my mind. "We all need friends in here. I can be a friend to you . . ." Man, those lines sickened me the first time I heard them.

For years I'd been talking the talk, assuming that I'd physically recognize when I finally experienced paranormal contact. But now, I knew it had already happened, and I just wasn't ready to accept or understand it back then. As a psychic, Chris was used to feeling and allowing stimuli to connect dots concerning matters of an other-worldly nature. Back in 2005, when I was feeling a pain in the same area, I'd assumed a medical explanation. But I was wrong.

On TV, you hear claims of people getting touched or pushed or scratched by entities. *Step in this room, get your hair pulled,* or *Old Man Bob is known to shove blondes!* But this wasn't a library or bed and breakfast. It was a prison. My hair wasn't tugged, nor was I gently pushed. I, too, had been grabbed in the balls. Eastern State Penitentiary had made me its bitch! 'We all need friends in here . . .'

As the understanding washed over me, the loose end to that story became clear. Back then, I was still a novice investigator. Even though I had brought devices to help me connect, I wasn't ready to accept that my body was the most basic device I could carry. Now, when I relate the concept to others, I can back it up with personal experience, and since then, I've learned to recognize it when it happens.

I've told this story at many universities and paranormal events. It never fails to get a laugh at key points, and those who were there for my realization still remind me of it from time to time. A colleague of mine on a popular television show even called me from Eastern State one night as they were filming to ask, "Hey, I heard you got touched down here—want to tell me about it?"

Yeah, the double entendre still makes me laugh. The touch may have been a bad one, but the experience was game-changing for me.

2

Learning To Fly

When I was a boy, I would have vivid dreams, often of places I'd never actually visited but was somehow familiar with. None of them were too detailed, but they represented types of places—such as "school" or "home." And sometimes, the dreams were scary. I'd see garish creatures that would fill me with dread. They never saw or chased me, but something told me to make myself scarce when they arrived.

Another important aspect of those dreams was my ability to fly. I ignored the laws of physics that restricted my waking hours and flew at will. All I had to do was think it. If I wanted to levitate off the ground, I could do so. Traveling between locations was easy, too; there was no actual passing of time involved. Often I would just find myself in some new place, having gotten there by sheer force of will. Thinking back on it, such an ability was amazing, but within the dream, it didn't even occur to me that I shouldn't be able to do so.

Such are the dreams of a boy who sees the world through a child's eyes. The universe is a wide and wonderful place with many incredible things to discover. My dreams intensified in high school. I didn't realize it then, but now I believe I know why.

***

I attended an all-boys Catholic high school where things were as strict as one might imagine. Having gone to public elementary and middle schools, the discipline (and the uniforms) took a bit of adjusting. We had religion class, masses for special days, and all sorts of events that involved the Church and our part in it. My parents were not overly religious, but they felt the school would give me the best education, and religion was just gravy on top of it all. As I learned about saints and Jesus and all things Heavenly in school, I sought knowledge about other things outside of school. I was always fascinated by the mysteries of our world—Stonehenge, Bigfoot, the Loch Ness Monster. I was also curious about magic and the powers of the mind. I seriously believed. So much so that I was too afraid to do the Bloody Mary challenge in the mirror—just in case!

As I progressed through high school, Scriptures seemed nothing more than stories, and that other stuff I'd been studying on my own seemed closer to the truth. Those other things were known as the occult—telekinesis, extrasensory perception, séances, and even astral travel—and they were considered subversive in the eyes of the Church. They were strictly forbidden and could not be openly discussed, much less looked into. But I did so anyway.

A couple of close friends shared my curiosity for occultism, and we would meet after school to read books on various subjects. I can still remember the smell of the pages, their yellow edges, the feel of the worn spines. What we discovered seemed obvious, like essential knowledge hidden in plain sight just waiting to be rediscovered. We pored through the various tomes trying to find our truth.

Astral travel really caught our attention. It seemed like the ultimate thrill ride, akin to a superpower. The ability to separate one's essence from their physical body and travel the world—nay, the universe—was very attractive. Of course, at the time, our field of vision was limited to the interests of teenage boys: advancing our station in the school social hierarchy, finding ways to amass some cash—and girls. Hell, maybe it was just girls. But we told ourselves differently. I think it all boiled down to power–feeling powerful during a time when so much was uncertain, and change was a daily companion and scary to confront. The ability to take back power was at the root of everything we researched, whether we were aware of it or not. It nestled into my subconscious as a lesson in humanity that I would draw upon in later years. During college, when I worked at a bookstore, I would see it in the eyes of hurting girls buying witchcraft books, hoping to force affection from guys who barely knew they existed. I've seen it also in those who try to mask uncertainty with the guise of faith.

We would lay on the floor of my friend Mike's bedroom, reciting the meditation that was supposed to calm our conscious minds and free our souls. It felt like a harmless exploration. The book didn't call for any candles, pentagrams, or sacrifices. It simply instructed that we open our minds and prepare for a trip. It was passive, peaceful even. I recall staring up at the ceiling, looking at the periwinkle walls, and tracing the lines where they met. I remember the instructions, which told me to imagine a hallway and a door we were supposed to step through and find a stairway. Farther and farther, more doors and more hallways. At one point, I heard a low rumble; it was our friend Justin snoring. That caused Mike to start giggling, snapping us back to reality, and another failed attempt.

But my dreams at night intensified. The places I'd visited began to have more detail. They felt more familiar each time. Flying became just like walking. I never gave it a second thought.

Time passed, and we got distracted and interested in other things as teenage boys do. Video games. Dungeons & Dragons. Girls. The astral attempts were forgotten, and the books shelved. Graduation came, and our little group of friends drifted apart as college life occupied our focus.

The pursuit of knowledge at the collegiate level (and returning to a co-ed environment) came with its own set of challenges. The boy who marveled at the wonders of the world had become the young man who questioned every tradition and tale he'd ever heard. But isn't that what college is about? Thinking that you know everything? I began disassociating myself from holiday practices, which seemed to have little purpose anymore. This translated into a general skepticism about most things, including work, school, and relationships.

After graduation, the humdrum routine of adulthood did not improve my outlook. If anything, it made me more of a cynic, and my dreams began to reflect this attitude. Once familiar places felt increasingly foreign. Then one night, I saw them—the creatures I'd seen in my younger days. They were tall, orange-brown in color, with fur or hair covering their entire body. I could never get a close look because any attempt to gaze directly at them caused a blur in my vision. It was almost as if they were camouflaging themselves on purpose. They traveled in packs, and it seemed to me their arms (if that's what they were) were always raised as they scurried along. Where a head should be, I saw only an open wound. Whether a maw or a gash, to look upon it, even peripherally, filled me with dread as it had in those early years. What did their return signal? Were they now aware of me? Were they coming for me?

I chose flight—which was no longer for travel but escape. The creatures seemed restricted to the ground, so the air was a safe space for me. I wasn't getting a restful night's sleep as these encounters became more common; hence, during the day, I was fatigued. The places I used to visit became infested with the creatures, and I found myself a tramp existing in the in-betweens. I was losing power over the situation.

One night, I came across another traveler, and we spent some time on "the road" together. I couldn't tell whether it was another dreamer or a facet of my subconscious, but it was nice to have company for once. Eventually, we could go no farther as the creatures blocked the path. We both agreed that up was the only option. Higher and higher, we rose until we reached the upper stratosphere. I could feel the cold air of space chilling my skin. I hesitated.

"What's wrong?" my companion asked.

"We're too high. If we go any higher, I'm afraid I won't be able to get back down!"

A terror ran through my veins. I couldn't go back down; I couldn't go farther up. I was stuck! And remaining in place was not an option . . .

I woke up with a rapidly fading memory of the experience, which the events of the day would subsequently bury deep within my psyche. I was completely unaware that I had just taken my last flight.

For many nights thereafter, my slumber was absent of any images. My astral self seemed to be holding its breath until one night it could hold it no more. There I was, on the road once again. Alone and wandering in a colorless landscape. A journey once filled with wonder and adventure had been stripped down to a march of confusion and uncertainty. Suddenly, I felt eyes on me. I stopped and looked around. The surroundings were barren, without any sign of the creatures, but I knew I was being watched and no longer safe on the road. I attempted to fly, but my feet remained firmly on the ground. I felt my breathing quicken. Time to fly—go! But nothing. I was grounded!

Jumping up, I felt a heaviness in my body that further accentuated the sad fact that I could no longer soar. Panic overtook me as I realized my watchers also were aware of my flightless state. Darkness began to close in. No form, no personality, just an absence was enveloping the surrounding hills and fields. It encountered no resistance and would be upon me in moments. This was it. With no avenue of escape, this would be the end. I looked up into the sky one more time as I tried to flex those old muscles. Again, nothing. I closed my eyes and prepared to accept whatever was next.

The alarm clock blared. I bolted straight up, my breathing still heavy, and wiped away a lingering tear. I felt an overwhelming sense of loss, as if something terrible had just happened. And in one way, it had. From that point forward, I never flew in my dreams again. I hadn't yet returned to my paranormal journey at the time, so the implications were shrouded from me. But even now, decades later, though I grasp the significance of my former astral travel, I've been unable to return to those heights, to those places.

I sincerely believe that in my younger years, my soul was exploring the astral plane, and to this day, I still dream of new locations, of new and familiar zones. But like an expat longing to return to his country, I am painfully aware of my apparent banishment. It's entirely possible that the restrictions which bind me are of my own creation—and as such, can only be dispelled by me—but for now, I remain in exile.

3

Advice from
Ed & Lorraine

I t was a month before The World's Largest Ghost Hunt would take place across the globe, and I found myself in Boyertown, PA, for a paranormal expo. A lot of people had shown up in the small town, and there was good energy all around. I was staying at a place called The Twin Turrets Inn, built in the 1800s and owned and run by the town's mayor. My room was one of those old suites containing a sitting area and a round turret portion overlooking the street. The plush bed may have been a four-poster at one time, and I was hesitant to touch the antique furniture, which appeared valuable to me. I did, however, make use of the writing desk. It had a foldaway top which I, of course, had to open and close a few times before that impulse was sated. Most of the furniture was dark stained wood with fern-colored, crest patterned upholstery. The dark orange walls were decorated with old paintings in ornate frames. It felt like the kind of room where one would sit with colleagues, smoke a cigar, and over a sifter of brandy muse how good it was to own land.

Whenever I found myself in such a fancy setting, I would make it a point to sit in silence for a while and soak in the atmosphere. It seemed wrong to turn on the television and disturb this classic ambiance, so it remained off for the duration of my stay. I was satisfied to be there and let the building talk to me, if it wished.

Before the event, I relaxed in my room and thought about the coming months, anxious about some big things in the pipeline. As I was pondering possibilities, I heard a few thuds in the hallway. Sticking my head out of the doorway, I saw a familiar figure turning the key to the room across from mine. He turned his head and chuckled.

"Hey Hippie, what are you doing here? I'm gonna call the cops!" John Zaffis teased. It was good to see the Old Man again—flat cap, solid sweatshirt, Members Only jacket, pulling a small suitcase on wheels. "You'd better get back on your island!" he continued to taunt.

"I'm gonna stab you, old man!"

John laughed warmly as we fell into our old routine, like Abbott & Costello. We'd seen each other on the circuit recently, but it was always so hectic. We hadn't had time to catch up in months with the schedules, the lectures, and the hunts. It had also been a while since we'd stayed in a place with the character and coziness of The Twin Turrets Inn.

At a convention or while filming our show, we had traditions on the road, and some things needed attending to. One of those was to always check in with each other after we got settled into our rooms—so we could find each other later, yes, but also to see whose room was bigger or had the most amenities. "Hey, Ziggity," I called across the hallway, "when you get your stuff in, come on over."

Interactions between John and I were usually pretty standard. The minutes of the meeting went like this: catch up about recent events, talk about the current event, trade gossip, and then anything else. This time, I also wanted to ask his advice about the upcoming World's Largest Ghost Hunt.

Earlier that year, a friend of mine had secured an official date for National Ghost Hunting Day. I had no idea one could do that, but as it turns out, there is an official committee in charge of managing such things. That's why every other day is National Cupcake Day, National Talk Like a Pirate Day, or something random like that. National Ghost Hunting Day was now on the list. Not to be confused with National Paranormal Day, mind you. Is there a difference?

When she told me about National Ghost Hunting Day, my friend also suggested that we do something to celebrate it, like maybe organizing a nationwide ghost hunt. I thought about it for a moment, then raised the ante. "Why not go global? If we're going to do something big, let's make it really BIG!" That is when the Bridge Experiment was born.

Maybe you've heard about the Bridge Experiment? The concept: fifty-two weekends out of the year saw countless paranormal groups investigating various locations. Questions were being asked; readings taken, and yet despite all this data, we'd gotten no further in advancing the field. I suspected that part of the problem was that all of these investigators were acting independently of each other. On National Ghost Hunting Day, if all groups work in tandem, perhaps we could increase the vibration, focus our intent, ask the Big Picture questions, and maybe—just maybe—have a better chance of getting solid answers. If they all asked the same questions at the same time, the combined energy might figuratively build a bridge to the Other Side, allowing for clearer communication than we'd ever experienced in isolation. Many locations, but one team, across the entire globe. What a concept! Could it be done?

Before long, we'd confirmed participation from groups in the United States, Australia, England, Ireland, and other nations. The night of the attempt would involve one team with members from ten countries across four continents! But I was unsure of what would happen. To my knowledge, nothing on this scale had ever been attempted. A part of me was fearful, concerned my enthusiasm might blind me to an unseen danger. That the penetration of the veil would rip a hole in the fabric of reality and wedge open a door that was supposed to remain closed. Would it be like *The Mist*, where horrendous creatures flooded into our plane of existence? Perhaps it would be like *Call of Cthulhu*, and we would awaken one of the Great Old Ones waiting to conquer our dimension.

This is why I wanted to talk to John. If anyone could advise me on the merits of exercising caution and staying away from the dark side of things, it was him. I asked him if The World's Largest Ghost Hunt was a good idea. He said he didn't see any problems with it and was excited to hear how it went. Then his eyes lit up as he reached into his pocket and brought out his smartphone.

"Why don't we ask right now?" he suggested.

Ziggity was old-fashioned. He liked his old toys, especially his Radio Shack brand hacked spirit box (the white one). But at the time of this conversation, he had become enamored with the phone app EchoVox, which he'd been using almost exclusively. Developed by Daniel Roberge, it was similar to a spirit box but did not rely on radio signals. Instead, it utilized several banks of random sound files and a hot mic on the device. As the app made its droning sounds, you would hear your voice echoing into the mix. It would then seem to fade away as if being flushed down a drain. Sometimes other voices would come back up, clear and bold and not your own.

So there we were in my room at Twin Turrets Inn, listening to the hypnotizing sounds of the phone app. Some voices were coming through, and John was trying to get them to identify themselves. It was a pretty standard session at the start. What happened next was anything but typical.

"Ed! Ed!" came the voice.

John nodded and smiled. "Yeah, we hear you," he answered.

In the past few months, whenever John would have an EchoVox session, one spirit consistently came through—his late uncle, Ed Warren. Ed would identify himself by repeating his name over and over until he was acknowledged. He would say other things in certain ways, known mainly to John, who knew Ed's mannerisms inside and out. It never failed to surprise me—watching a living legend converse with a deceased one—and the magnitude of the moment was not lost on me.

Ed had even come across during my own recent investigations. I didn't know why, for I had never had the chance to meet him while he was alive. When I mentioned this to John, he simply said, "Oh, he knows who you are, kid." That statement was equal parts scary and flattering. It made me wonder who else was watching. We were about to find out.

John invited me to ask about The World's Largest Ghost Hunt. I took a moment to phrase my question clearly, then asked if the endeavor was a good idea and if there could be any danger. We listened carefully as the response came back: "Good." I looked at John. He nodded. I asked again to be sure, and the response came back in the same voice. "Good."

I felt a sense of relief as I leaned back in my chair and allowed myself to relax—until I heard another voice chime in: "Be careful."

I straightened up and turned my head to hear better. The voice sounded familiar. John took notice of my posture and caught on immediately.

"Ahhh, what did ya hear, kiddo?"

I looked at him, unsure if I should vocalize what I was thinking. I was pretty sure I knew who the voice was coming from, but as I understood things, that was impossible. The Old Man knew exactly what was on my mind and urged me to speak it.

"John, I don't know how this could be possible, but"—he began nodding his head as I stammered—"that sounds like Lorraine. But how can that be?"

A pregnant pause followed. For a moment, I worried I'd said something foolish. John looked down and tugged at the hairs on his chin, as he did while deep in thought.

"No, you heard correctly," John confirmed. "Lorraine is quite gifted."

I knew it! I'd heard her voice, her tone, her cadence—but Lorraine Warren was still alive, so I was having trouble reconciling the truth behind it. Now, here is the funny thing about John Zaffis: he is a great repository of paranormal knowledge and has seen much and experienced even more, but that knowledge does not come out easily. John teaches by letting you conclude yourself and then confirms it once you arrive there. This moment was no different.

"I didn't want to assume anything, but . . ." John could see by my expression where I was going. "Could it be, because of her ability and her age, that she's got one foot in and one foot out?"

He nodded in the affirmative, then continued to tug at his beard as he stared at his phone. The conversation that followed was brief, as it often was when learning a new fact from John. I had many questions, but it was usually prudent to take small bites when digesting such a big revelation. Lorraine Warren was in her late eighties at the time, and, despite her renewed notoriety due to the *Conjuring* movies, she had begun to slow down. I had guessed that her psychic ability combined with her waning corporeal journey would allow her to communicate as spirit did. But was she asleep when it happened? Was it an unconscious action? Did Ed have anything to do with it? I had so many questions. Questions for which I still lack answers.

What the experience did do was assure me that The World's Largest Ghost Hunt would be something positive. Sure, many others stood in my corner supporting the experiment, but having Ed and Lorraine Warren weigh-in was huge. Their names have become legend. Their contributions to the paranormal field are immeasurable. These two were pounding the pavement and doing The Work a long time before it was fashionable. Were they saints? Not even close. They were regular human beings with flaws and vices, yet they took it upon themselves to navigate generally uncharted waters to try and help those around them with their paranormal problems.

While they gained notoriety for their efforts, Ed and Lorraine also were under intense scrutiny from media and other naysayers. For every person that applauded them, a hundred others doubted them. They operated in a time before *Ghostbusters*, before the paranormal reality TV explosion, before social media, a time when the words of a newspaper reporter would define the impression the public had about you. With many famous cases that would later be turned into movies under their belts, they continued to help people until the end of their lives. They chose their path, and it seemed that choice was not hindered by death. By watching over John and other investigators, they, in their way, are still doing The Work. And it's comforting to know.

When such huge figures pass on, there is always the feeling that a repository of knowledge has been lost. In this case, that knowledge lives on, and as long as we allow ourselves to listen, we'll hear their guidance.

***

The Bridge Experiment was conducted on October 1st, 2016, coordinated from a command center in Lexington, KY. It was the first occurrence of The World's Largest Ghost Hunt on National Ghost Hunting Day. It went as smoothly as a global event relying on untested teleconference software could. There were no casualties, and no monsters jumped through any open portals to our world, which were definite signs of success. What made it even better was the way all the teams around the globe worked in tandem—proof that it could be done. I hosted the experiment for the first two years, then stepped back. The event has continued to grow, and the concept of "One Team, Many Places" hopefully has taken hold in the minds of investigators around the world.

I'm now convinced that those on both sides of the veil are working to establish open communication, and I've learned the importance of consulting investigators who've gone before me. Sure, I still sometimes second guess my role in it all, but given the source of that lesson, I find myself in excellent company.

4

It's in the Cards

’ve been told by many that the Universe has a plan for us. To know what that is, we just need to listen. Yet, I wasn't always ready to do so. It took me many years, and many ignored messages to accept such a concept. Looking back, I have no idea how many instances there were, but I do recall one where a messenger was dispatched to tell me directly.

***

I spent eleven years working at Bartle Bogle Hegarty (BBH), an ad agency in Manhattan. It was a fun job, a challenging job, a tough job. I'd held several since college, but this was the first steady one, and it shaped much of what was to come in my life. The agency was British, and this was their first office in the States. As such, much of the culture originated from their home office in London. Every year included a day of relaxation and pampering to thank their employees. Each branch usually celebrated their own day, but from time to time, the whole worldwide company would gather at once with the motto: One Agency. Many Locations. That seed would grow into a mode of thinking I would later harvest during The World's Largest Ghost Hunt.

This year saw the New York branch posted up at a country club in Mamaroneck doing what they did best, making even the most mundane of activities look cool. It was one thing I always found fascinating about working there, but in hindsight, it all made sense. We were in the business of selling an image and the least we could do at any given moment was embody that image. Along with drinks and food, there were always some fun activities to engage in during these day-long soirees. Be it hitting the links, acting silly in a photo booth, dipping into the pool, or participating in group activities (to call them team building would be too formal a moniker at these events). There was never a dull moment on the docket. One year, I recall a 45-minute rendition of "We Are Family" performed by Sister Sledge, which delighted and eventually confused us. Another year, a curtain wall that had divided the ballroom dropped to reveal Blondie launching into a killer set that echoes in my mind to this day. I was mere feet from Deborah Harry. To those gathered, it was as if she were singing to each of us individually. The agency never spared an expense to entertain. This particular year, they had flown in a tarot card reader who, I'd been told, was Oprah Winfrey's personal reader. This seer to the stars would turn the cards for whoever wished to gaze into their future.

At this point, I was already doing *Scared on Staten Island* with my friends, but my paranormal journey was in its early stages, and I was at peak levels of skepticism. The world, however, had become a confusing and unsettling place, and with the events of 9/11 and the Great Northeast Blackout still fresh in my memory, I felt willing to give tarot card reading a chance. Despite my skeptical nature, I was also open-minded.

I can remember the temperature that day. I can remember the way the sun played off the concrete by the pool. I can remember the exit I took off the highway to get to the event. Many details I can recall, but for the life of me, I can't remember the moments leading up to me sitting at her table or even what she looked like. My brain fills out the forgotten details with stereotypical tropes of a tarot card reader's appearance. It could have been Miss Cleo sitting across from me. I do remember my determination to offer a blank surface; she would get absolutely nothing from my facial expression or my posture. I tried to be as neutral as possible. Now don't get me wrong; I wasn't doing this to be difficult or antagonistic, but as a skeptic, I wanted to eliminate as many cues as possible to prevent a cold reading. I had my poker face on and would be on the lookout for vague generalizations. Horoscope logic that could be applied to anyone anywhere would not pass my test. Additionally, if you come with a pedigree that includes Oprah Winfrey, you're setting a high bar. I wasn't going to accept anything less than amazing from Miss What-everHerNameWas (yes, in hindsight, I wish I'd paid more attention to that simple detail).

"Do you have any questions for me?" she asked in an accent I suspect has been manufactured by my memory.

"No, nothing specific. I'm just curious to see what you get," I replied.

One by one, she turned over the cards. She would explain what they were and what they could mean to me. I sat still and expression-less.

"What's this? You're going to be on television," she said as she laid a card down across another.

I did my best not to react. My first thought was, *I seriously doubt that*, followed by, *well, I am doing the cable access show*. Eventually, I would transfer to the BBH broadcast department, but at the time, I was a graphic artist in the studio. How did she make the connection to TV? I broke my stoic mask to raise an eyebrow in implied disbe-lief.

"Yes, it's going to be a national TV show. You're going to do quite well," she continued.

My mind raged against the news while my ego celebrated it. To be frank, I was probably the least cool person at the gathering. I could see plenty of others at the agency making it onto TV and doing well, but not me. In fact, one of my colleagues would go on to co-host *Germany's Next Top Model* with Heidi Klum. Now that made sense—that guy had rock star vibes, and everything he did was in-credibly cool. But me?

Sitting poolside with this cartomancer, I had no idea what she could be seeing to indicate such a prediction. My humble cable access show was not something I spoke about to my co-workers, so they couldn't have informed her. Nor was I a searchable entity on Google or IMDb yet. I just had to take her at her word. I mean, this method of fortune-telling was not set in stone, and given my state of open-ness at the time, I was not ready to see what she saw until much later. I could tell people I was read by Oprah's tarot reader, and that be-came the extent of the anecdote. It wasn't until many years later that her vision became a reality, and rounded out this story. Yet, there was still one last piece to the session that sticks out to this day.

"But who is this?" she asked, a slight hint of concern in her voice as she pointed to a final card on top of the others. I leaned forward to examine it closer. I don't remember the card, but I remember feeling a chill, like a bucket of cold water had been dumped over me. It was as if the Universe was warning me: this future comes at a price. As it always does.

"They're standing in a doorway, between you and what I told you before," she added.

What was this now? I'd barely had a moment to enjoy the possible good news; now, someone was coming to rain on my parade.

"Can you clarify?" I asked.

"Do you know who this is?" she countered. Her tone made the question feel more like an accusation. "Who is this?" she repeated.

Now I was getting a little paranoid, like when a cop pulls you over and asks routine questions. I was under the microscope.

She described the person as someone I knew or would come to know who would stand in the way of my progress. She was unclear if it would be an adversary or someone that diverted me from my path unknowingly. Either way, it seemed to disturb her.

I racked my brain to figure out who it could be. A friend? A girlfriend? A colleague? Someone I had yet to meet? The exercise unnerved me. There was no way to positively identify the person.

I returned to the party with a shadow following me. I was and still am a big believer in Free Will and the invalidity of Absolute Destiny, but hearing that there may be someone out there trying to stop you is never welcome news. To this day, I wonder if I have yet encountered that blocking force. I can assign that role to several people, but the specific one Oprah's reader saw, I may never know.

As for the message delivered, did it reach me? A woman told me I would end up on TV years before it happened, but given a long enough timeline, would it have happened anyway? Was she really seeing that moment in time?

I accept my role in this—I was producing a show of my own, with ambitions to go higher. She couldn't have known it specifically, but my trajectory was set. I could have laid it all down and gone a different direction, but I didn't. Was that choice or consequence?

I've since had many encounters with psychics and seers of all varieties. Some tell me about my supposed past lives. Others tell me of their connection to me across time. A few offer warnings and a couple have been specific about events. No matter what the report, I know that none of them are Gospel.

Are there indeed messengers of the Universe? The jury is still out about that one. If there is a Plan, I remain unaware. But I am open to the possibility and await the next messenger.

5

The Warning Hand

There is a saying in demonology that has always stuck with me: When you study evil, evil studies you. To land on the radar of something malevolent was never one of my goals when I entered into the paranormal. But I suppose that if you do The Work long enough, such an outcome is inevitable. Not every case will have you meeting Casper the Friendly Ghost. In fact, many investigations turn up nothing, and if you encounter anything at all, it will likely be neutral. So, what usually concerns investigators most is not encountering evil but picking up attachments. An attachment, in this context, is a supernatural stowaway, a spiritual souvenir that you did not intend to return with.

That being said, I feel pretty lucky to have never brought anything home with me. If I had snagged any attachments, I believe they resolved themselves quickly. I'd always quipped that spirits would get quite bored following me home and would search out more interesting targets.

I made that exact joke one weekend at an event in Ohio. I don't remember the venue, but I do recall the drive home. Events are often very draining for me. They involve long hours and late nights, with many miles to traverse in between. No matter how enjoyable or enlightening the time, the trip home is often done on autopilot. Farmhouses and silos along twisty country roads usually keep me interested, but once I hit an interstate, the details and scenery become quite humdrum. Having a nearby goal, like a stop at Sheetz for food or gas, always helps to keep me awake. But without a mission, those highway lines conspire against me. The exit signs and mile markers all begin to blur.

I was getting older and less resilient at the time of this event, but I chose to roll the dice another time, driving back to Staten Island in the late afternoon, completely exhausted. Only this time, I knew better than to tempt fate. Chalk it up to weariness or wisdom, but I knew it was time to take a break. I wasn't exactly sure where I was, just nowhere near home. And then my phone chimed, alerting me to a waiting message.

It was from a colleague who had seen my posts online about the event and was reaching out to see how it went. What fortuitous timing! As luck would have it, they were staying nearby, and food was currently being prepared. A minor detour would have me there in time for supper. The sun was setting, and the last thing I wanted to do was drive in the dark while I was fatigued. Instead, I would cap off a good weekend in an unexpected way by visiting with an old friend. It's good to have friends!

Al was an investigator steeped in the natural end of The Work, one who always managed to fascinate and scare me with the stories of the cases he was working on. In the early days, I was extremely skeptical of his reports, but in time, I realized he was far more experienced. Our paths were disparate, but our common bond was wanting to make a difference. Al brought an intense determination to everything he did, and it kicked into high gear while working on a case. As it turned out, he was working a live-in case at that very house.

After I arrived, we spent time talking about what we'd been up to and who we'd recently run into, as well as the latest news. Along with several of his housemates, we supped and laughed as we all traded stories. It was a jovial experience that made it easy to forget I was stepping into an active investigation.

As always, Al wanted to immerse himself into the case to evaluate better how to help. He lived there with three others: Mike and Jenn (a couple) and an elderly gentleman, Roger. They seemed like nice people. I didn't ask any questions about the activity occurring, and no details were offered. Coming off an event, I still had to detox from ghost stories myself, so it was nice to avoid any new ones. The good company melted some of the fatigue away and made me feel like I could hit the road again. I began to shift in my seat and started the preambles of my exit.

"Nonsense," Al said. "You can go home in the morning when you're properly rested." I wanted to get home, but the thought of making the trek across Pennsylvania in the dark did not thrill me. I agreed to stand down for the night.

Knowing that I would be resuming my drive in the morning allowed me to relax. Drowsiness once again crept over me. The small guest room I would be staying in was sparse, and I preferred it that way. I'd always felt a little uncomfortable in someone else's room, especially if I didn't know them well. An unused spare bedroom was a different story.

I changed into sleep clothes and put my worn ones in my travel bag on the floor, next to my boots. The hour was late, and the others had already retired to their rooms, save for Roger, who slept on the couch. He needed the television on to fall asleep, and at his age, he needed it loud. Every late-night commercial for sex chat lines and accident lawyers came through the wall with perfect clarity. I could hear him changing channels, and yet he managed to find all the same commercials. I'm the kind of person who prefers silence to fall asleep. But I was a guest in this house and was not going to say a thing. I could just put a pillow over my ears when I lay down. That's when I noticed I had none.

With impeccable timing once again, Al poked his head into the room. "You all good? Need anything before I turn in?"

"Actually, I could use a pillow, if you don't mind," I replied.

"I'll ask Jenn for one when she gets out of the bathroom," Al said.

We talked as we waited—the mundane chit-chat of two tired people who had already mentally checked out for the night. Out in the living room, I could hear that Roger had settled on a movie, although I wasn't sure which one. The score was unfamiliar.

"I'm going to go grab a quick smoke, and then we'll get you sorted out," Al informed me. Smokers and their habits. I nodded and smiled as he ducked out of the room. Sitting on the edge of the bed, I began to feel a little antsy. At this point, all I wanted to do was lay down and get some sleep. I was thankful they had room for me, but I was getting cranky. I took a deep, cleansing breath and began to calm down. Then I heard a rustling by the window.

Night had fallen, and there was no detail to be seen beyond the curtain, only darkness. The window itself was open a few inches, just enough to let in some air–along with a tiny moth. I watched it as it fluttered from the opening and headed for my bag. "SHOO!" I hissed as I tried to alter its flight path with my foot. Woods surrounded the house in every direction. You'd think the moth would be able to find somewhere other than my bag to occupy its short life. Another ungraceful swipe of my leg got it to fly out the door and into the hallway. *Go keep Roger company*, I thought.

Suddenly a gunshot blared out! The sound momentarily startled me until I realized it had come from whatever movie Roger had settled upon. My senses suddenly sharp; I felt the penetrating vibrations of a military march. The music surged then ebbed as dialogue took over and became too low for me to hear. My heart was beating faster. I rubbed my cold hands together to try to increase circulation.

Again, I heard rustling by the window. Another moth fluttered in. I was about to get up and capture it when I found myself frozen! My muscles refused to heed the commands of my brain. I could only stare as the curtains began to sway. The room became an icebox as the temperature plunged. The light in the corner dimmed slightly. The fight or flight response had kicked in, but I was powerless to do either.

I heard a low rumble, but it wasn't coming from the living room. Then I saw it . . . fingers protruded from out of the darkness and overlapped the curtain. A dark, grey hand pulled the fabric to the left, exposing nothing discernible beyond it, just more darkness. A voice, deep and gruff sounding like it came from below the ground, evolved from the rumble.

"You have fifteen minutes to get out of this house. I'm going to fucking kill you."

The words plunged me into a panic that was heightened by my inability to defend myself. From the living room, the sounds of machine-gun fire and explosions accented the threat. I could hear the cries of dying soldiers, and for a moment, the sound seemed to be coming from within my room.

The grey hand withdrew from the window, and suddenly I was able to move again!

I sprang into action—swiftly changing back into my street clothes and throwing on my boots. Trying to work through the fear, my mind was burning with the limited details I struggled to process. What did I just witness? One of the housemates having some fun at my expense? A neighbor or friend popping by in morbid fashion? The voice hadn't sounded like anyone I'd heard that evening. It was strong and forceful but with a raspy, gravelly quality, like an old man who had seen things in his life. Things like war and death. Could it have been Roger? Was he annoyed that I was in his house—did I overstay my welcome or somehow offend him earlier? Beyond the weight of the words, I had also picked up something else: Rage.

As if cued by my awareness, something started pounding on the side of the house! It wasn't a gentle knock or an accidental hit—it was a deliberate banging, the physical threat to accompany the words still ringing in my ears.

Though I was afraid it would try to get in through the window, I did not attempt to get closer or survey the exterior. To do so would've put me in a prone position. Beyond the noise from the television, the house was quiet. If there was someone (or something) outside, would it try to come in another way? I grabbed my bag and prepared to make tracks. Clearly, my delayed response was flight.

But where was Al? If he had gone outside to have a cigarette, whatever was out there would have encountered him. The absence of non-cinematic voices filled me with dread. This wasn't a movie or a video game. I actually feared for my life.

The voice at the window had not come from a human. Somewhere in the depths of my being, I knew this, but the straight jacket of logic refused to accept it. There had to be a rational explanation that would involve someone I could negotiate with, fight with, or at the very least run past! How was it that I was the only person in the house reacting to this right now? Where the hell was Al?

Standing in the doorway of the guest room, I steeled myself for what I might find beyond it. I looked back at the window and saw only blackness, and then, taking a deep breath, stepped out into the hallway. Ahead of me, in the kitchen, a figure stepped into view—it was Al!

He saw the look on my face and immediately switched into work mode.

"What's wrong?" he asked.

"Someone at the window just threatened to kill me," I replied. Saying it out loud felt odd to me—as if I were a child telling a parent about a bad dream.

His response simultaneously calmed and upset me. With confidence and resolve befitting someone who had tilted with this darkness before, he nodded and wordlessly walked back outside. Alone in the kitchen, I waited for what I assumed would be the sounds of an argument. At this point, I was still hoping for a human explanation.

The kitchen was an open space adjacent to the living room where Roger still slumbered on the couch. I crept over to make sure he was still breathing. A loud snore erupted, providing proof of life. The movie providing the audio backdrop to my unfolding drama was *We Were Soldiers*, which starred Mel Gibson. I'd never seen it before, but the scenes and soundtrack seemed to mirror my feelings.

As I waited for Al to return, I surveyed the area. Both the kitchen and living room were flanked by large windows, which by day offered a lovely view of the surrounding woods but by night showed nothing but sheets of black. A small alcove off the kitchen led into a mudroom that exited to the outside. I felt exposed as if I were in a menagerie, trapped and unable to hide.

Long moments passed, and still, I waited. Feeling helpless in the face of potential danger made each second seem like an agonizing eternity. What was taking Al so long, and why couldn't I hear anything beyond the television?

My mind raced with horrible possibilities. In a wilderness such as this, almost everyone owned guns. Did this visitor have a problem with Roger or Al or anyone else in the house, or was he just a random villain? Unarmed, I would be little help if this came down to a shootout, and law enforcement was nowhere nearby.

My only measure of actual time passing was the movie. Scene after scene played out as I became increasingly aware of my need to do something other than standing there waiting. I crouched down low and made my way to the mudroom door. Peeking through the screen, I could make out blurry images of cars parked beside the house. Moonlight illuminated the pathway to potential freedom, and I began to plot out my next steps.

I strained to hear all I could, but it was eerily quiet outside. Given what I had experienced and the way Al strode off, I assumed there would be some sort of confrontation and that it would be easy to hear. No such luck. The silence only served to fix my feet to the ground once again as the suffocating tendrils of terror wrapped around my throat. I silently cursed my apparent cowardice. If Al had encountered something violent out there, he could be hurt and in need at that very moment, and there I was cowering amongst the gardening tools! Come on, Brian, buck up!

I grabbed the first thing I saw, a red plastic broom, and prepared to make my move. I could see my car but not the front of the house, where I expected to find my friend. The plan was to run over to my vehicle, take cover, and then re-evaluate the situation. I had a flimsy cleaning tool clutched tightly in my grasp, preparing to pit it against a possible firearm—or worse, as my imagination continued to evolve the scene. Every horror movie I'd ever seen began to flip through my mind.

I leaned back and took one last look into the living room. Roger slept like the dead, unaware of all of it. Mike and Jenn had not made a peep from their room either. For a household experiencing paranormal activity, they seemed to all be heavy sleepers!

It was time to act. I slowly pushed open the screen door, doing my best to manage the squeak of the hinges. A rush of adrenaline moved me forward. Crisp night air filled my lungs. The moon shone brighter than expected, and I could see the whole landscape tinted in blue: the pine forest on all sides, the mountains beyond, the winding dirt road that led out of the clearing, and most importantly, my car. Despite all this visual detail, the one thing still missing was sound. The forest was still. No denizen of the wild howled or cried. Only the sound of my breathing and the pounding of my pulse kept me from thinking I'd gone deaf. I was out of the house. I had made the first steps. Now I just had to keep going. I'm coming, Al, hang on!

Staying low to the ground, I scampered towards the car as the sound of my boots crunching gravel echoed into the night. My efforts to be stealthy were meeting with some resistance. Reaching my vehicle, I opened the door and quickly locked myself inside. I felt somewhat safer but knew there was more I had to do.

Peering through the windshield, I surveyed the house. The front of the rancher was understated and only distinguished from the mudroom entrance by a larger main door and the house number adorning it. A modest lawn stretched some fifty feet out before it met the tree line. Just beyond the front door was the living room where Roger lay. Several feet to the right was a pile of wood by the guest bedroom window. I saw no sign of the intruder or Al.

Where could he have gone? From my vehicular vantage point, I saw no evidence of a struggle or even simple proof that anyone had been out there. I was put to a decision—do I stay and investigate further, or do I start the car and get the hell out of there?

Moments later, my car turned onto the country road that led to the interstate, a dust trail chasing behind, rising into the night sky. The decision had been quick and, despite the nagging shame I felt, each mile I traveled made me feel safer. I met my own gaze in the rearview mirror and saw a stranger looking back. Having never been in this situation before, it was impossible to compare my performance to another. Fear still ran through my veins and kept my foot firmly pressed on the gas pedal. As I navigated back onto the highway, I sent Al a quick text, telling him I'd left and to contact me at once.

Previously, my thoughts had been bathed in bloody images of what might happen to me if I stuck around. Now, the main character in my musings was Al, and the future headlines became more and more grisly.

Nine minutes passed before my phone chimed and ended my chilling sentence. Al was okay! He had gone next door to rouse a neighbor and check out the area. I was so relieved to get the message that I laughed out loud—the type of laughter that comes after an ordeal, a nervous yet cleansing expulsion of emotion.

We compared notes on the evening. I gave Al my perspective of the occurrence as well as my assumptions about its source. He then filled me in on his half. After heading outside, he and a couple of neighbors (yes, with shotguns) had patrolled the outside of the house as well as the surrounding area to see if they could find anything to corroborate my story. As experienced outdoorsmen, their tracking skills, even at night, were something I did not need to question. Much to my dismay, they found nothing. Not a single piece of evidence to show that someone had been outside that window. In fact, the pile of firewood I had observed would have made it nearly impossible for anyone to get close to the window, let alone insert a hand. As Al recounted that to me, I recalled the phantom hand and the banging I'd heard. It raised more questions than answers.

The house was the site of an ongoing investigation. Had I angered whatever was affecting the family? As far as the standard "get out" responses went, this one was pretty specific. During my exodus, I leaned towards a human explanation, perhaps to anchor my mind in the corporeal. But the facts, as told to me by my friend, shifted the coming conclusion. With no tracks, nothing disturbed, and only my description of what happened to weigh in on, I realized my original feelings were correct. As my favorite fictional consulting detective famously stated, "Once you eliminate the impossible, whatever remains, however improbable, must be the truth." Check and check. I'd had a supernatural experience. Ironically, it wasn't during an event or on an investigation but during my downtime. The Universe was not without its keen sense of timing.

Message delivered!

The weight on my heart had lifted after I found out Al was safe and no one had been hurt, but I couldn't help feeling like things were not okay. Such incidents cause ripples. What would they affect, and where would they reverberate?

The trek across Pennsylvania was normally a straight six-hour shot. I'd already been an hour or so in when I'd made my detour, and now traveling with haste along an empty highway, one would assume I'd make excellent time. But that was not to be my fate. After the initial shock and excitement wore off, fatigue once again gripped me. I swerved and drifted. I stopped at rest stops. I pulled off onto dark side roads to attempt quick naps, but I'd only find myself awake minutes later, back on the road, exhausted and eager for home. It was like an aftershock of torment—the torture of wanting nothing but to lie in your own bed but being painfully far from it. That was my trip home, a trip that took just over ten hours from the flash point.

It was like experiencing altered states. I even wondered if I'd made it out of that ranch house at all. Had I tarried too long and allowed my fifteen minutes to expire (a double entendre that I muse about often), resulting in the entity carrying out its promise? Perhaps it was only my consciousness racing down that highway as my body remained immobile, somewhere in that car park. One of my favorite ghost stories is about the man who never reached home, a trope wherein travelers would come across him urgently trying to ask directions but never believing them when told. His journey was an eternal one, an endless loop that would forever have him just out of reach of the rest he sought. I wondered if I now shared a similar fate. Did anyone at the gas stations and rest stops see me? Was I now on an odyssey of my own?

To this day, I still have no concrete answers about what I experienced that night. I recently spoke to Al and revisited the incident with him. I got no further clarity on what happened, but I did get some additional information. The case Al was working on has been closed for some time now. About a year after my visit, Roger passed on. Upon hearing this, I paused and asked a delicate question: "Al, do you think they got him?"

I knew whatever was haunting that place was dark—Al had told me as much. So it seemed relevant to ask the manner of Roger's death. Was it a peaceful passing, or did the entities finally complete their endgame? In the short time that I had been exposed to the man, I detected a sense of confidence, a way about him that informed me he was used to being counted on. Even in his elder state, I sensed strength of character. When I thought of Roger, I thought of a soldier, ready and prepared to defend others at all costs. Perhaps he'd died fighting one last battle.

Al told me that Roger would have restless nights and talk or even cry out in his sleep. Something was playing out in the moments between consciousness and slumber. He had a burden made heavier by the phantoms feeding on his past, which seemed to make a certain sense. Imagine a pack of predators in the wild, gorging on a recent kill. If you approached, they would snarl and try to chase you away. If you got too close, you might become next on the menu. That night I may have stumbled too close to a feeding ground.

I just hope that in his final moments, Roger didn't give up. If it was his time to go, it was his time to go, but I imagine he died with his boots on. I'd say rest in peace, but given everything I've learned over the years, it seems there is no true rest. He's off on the next phase, the next adventure. So perhaps bon voyage is more appropriate.

All my instincts were put to use that night at Roger's place. As I write these words, I access those feelings and images again. They return in full color and clarity. The grand facade of who I thought I was or wanted to be was put up against the reality of my actions. So, soon after, I chose to repress it—until now. As I tell people who criticize paranormal shows from the safety of their couches: It's one thing to see a retelling of paranormal activity, but it's another thing when something paranormal addresses you specifically with life-threatening vehemence! They often scoff and say they'd handle things differently. Well, I've now been on both sides of that equation and learned a lesson that will burn in me for the rest of my days.

There is one thought that does descend upon me from time to time in those quiet, dark hours of the night; the hours you spend alone with your thoughts and insecurities. What I contemplate is this:

As I've thought about the Warning Hand over the years, has that entity been thinking about me? When you study evil, evil studies you.

I do believe I received a warning that night. Perhaps it was a test. If so, I don't think I did very well. Looking back, I can't help but wonder what Roger would have done in my position—what he might have been doing every night in that house. If my impression of him is correct, it would behoove me to be more like him. So down the line, when someone has cause to write their anecdote about me, they can say I went out with my boots on.

6

The Circle of Fire

Turn on the television. Flip through the channels. Eventually, you'll come across a ghost hunting show. Watch long enough, and you'll view a demonic case, with all the paranormal activity assigned to one of Hell's minions. A voice, a feeling, something thrown off a shelf, or the dreaded three scratches across the back. "It's a demon!" they'll cry. Get out the holy water, call in the exorcist—but wait, we don't want to dispel the demon doing wonders for our ratings!

Can you blame them? It's not the investigators' fault; it's the producers, the network. They know what sells. They know what gets people on all ends of the belief spectrum to tune in, either to be captivated by the hunt or to scoff at the silliness of the on-screen antics. If you're a black shirt (my term for a proud member of a paranormal group), you raise an eyebrow at the episode, probably for various reasons. I know I still do. The demonic is a heavy topic. How many entities pull out ID cards and confirm which union they're in?

I was raised Catholic, so the concept of demons does resonate with me. As a paranormal investigator, I feel like I can handle spirits and ghosts. What's the worst that could happen? As we've already noted, an attachment, or perhaps some manageable negativity for a brief time. But dealing with the demonic has ramifications for my soul—that great unknown yet invaluable asset we all possess. That scares me. How can a puny human like me battle entities that possess such hatred and have all the time in the world to enact their machinations against us? It's mind-boggling. Yet seldom does an event go by without some black shirt, two months into The Work, claiming they handle demonic cases all the time. Oh, sure, it's as simple as separating your clothes for the wash. No worries, they've watched "(Insert Ghost Show Here)" so they can handle it. It frustrates me even as I write this. I have no ire towards my colleagues on the shows that frequently portray demonic activity, but they do create the perception that every other case out there is demonic and that the world is filling up with evil. But in my almost twenty years as a paranormal investigator, I have only ever worked one case that I believe was demonic. It was at a place known as The Grand Midway Hotel.

I came to Windber, PA, in the summer of 2009. The town was a small sleepy one nested between mountains. As such, it was always ten degrees colder than the other towns around it. Windber was founded by and named for the Berwind-White Coal Mining Company (BWMC) in the late 1800s when the mining boom in Pennsylvania had created a culture of industry. In some way or another, everyone in Windber owed their existence to that company, although the same could be said for more than just the locals.

Requiring more able-bodied men to work in the mines, the BWMC sent representatives over to Europe to recruit whomever they could. Workers were promised a home as well as a handsome starting bonus for crossing the Atlantic to work in Pennsylvania, and

they were told they could soon bring their families. It sounded too good to be true—and as such stories tend to go, it was.

The men came in droves, all looking to make a better life for themselves in America. After getting off the boat in New York, they would board the train to Windber. In fact, the tracks led directly to what was then called The Midway Hotel, owned by the BWMC. But instead of hearing a welcome message, the disembarking miners were briefed on an unfortunate setback. They were told that the houses they'd been promised were not ready yet, but not to despair—they would all be put up at the hotel for a bare minimum cost, which would be deducted from their starting bonuses. And so it was that the crew of the Berwind-White Mining Company "temporarily" took residence at The Midway Hotel. What could go wrong?

"You haul sixteen tons, and what do you get? Another day older and deeper in debt," crooned the Paul Robeson song. That's how it went for the men at The Midway. They would work their shifts in the mine and then return to the hotel. Without the responsibilities of family to occupy them during the off-hours, the vices of downtime took over. Between gambling, drinking, and women, the men frittered away their pay until none was left. To afford to stay at the hotel meant owing the company and working to settle their growing debt. What had begun as a promise of prosperity turned into de facto slavery. Morale sunk, and uncertainty cast a dark shadow over the workers. There was no way to fight the company; there were no unions yet, and organizations such as the Molly Maguires were not a factor. Worse, anyone who tried to organize the men or speak up against the conditions allegedly disappeared. Rumor had it that many of those men ended up buried beneath the hotel.

The mining industry in Windber eventually dried up and left those who remained struggling to survive. As seen in many towns that rise and fall around a specific employer, Windber faced obliteration. But years of debauchery and despair at The Midway had perhaps left a deeper wound, one that would fester throughout the decades. After the mines closed, the hotel eventually did as well, becoming a pharmacy and even a disco before it sat abandoned for over ten years.

Enter Blair Murphy. A creative in Hollywood, Blair had tried his hand in production but found it unfulfilling. His destiny lay on a different road, and like Tyler Durden in *Fight Club*, he chose to strike out on his own and move into an old, abandoned hotel in the middle of nowhere, a hotel he purchased on eBay for the sum of $11,000.

Yes, you read that right. The hotel was severely dilapidated, but nevertheless, Blair was drawn to it, and the first thing he did was rename it The Grand Midway Hotel.

Blair's "Project Mayhem" at The Grand Midway was not to be organized public chaos but rather an encouragement of the arts. He envisioned a place where artists of all kinds—musicians, poets, painters, and writers—could come and just be. A place that would foster creativity in whatever outlet they chose. But first, there was work to be done. The hotel's notorious reputation was as daunting as its structural imperfections, not to mention the residual negative energy left behind by the miners. Blair spent his first two years residing on the first floor, in the main bar area, as he removed and repaired whatever he could. The winters were cold, the summers were hot, but he persevered. By his own admission, the place was creepy, but having been raised by morticians, he was unfazed by such things. He was determined to realize his dream one way or another.

Eventually, Blair was able to inhabit the upper stories of the 33-room hotel. Many artists soon joined him. They moved into the rooms as if Blair were curating a collection of creatives. Little by little, his vision was taking shape. Adding to the strange energy of the place was an imaginative vibe that created a quirkiness all its own. Blair would hold events dedicated to Jack Kerouac and Dracula that, in turn, attracted more like-minded guests.

One such person was a painter named Dylan. His involvement in this story is cursory but all-important to the outcome. As with many artists, he dabbled in addictive substances intending to spur his creativity, but they ultimately took him to dark places. Add to that a peculiar predilection for a form of body suspension in which he would get into a special suit and hang from the ceiling. As a painter, he was always looking to broaden his horizons and gain inspiration from different experiences and states of mind. So there he would be, in his room, in the summer, hanging from chains attached to his bodysuit and sweating it out. The heat baked his body, the drugs baked his mind, and he journeyed to places known only to him. Then he'd paint whatever he saw.

As time passed, Dylan's paintings began to take on a darker tone, and a specific figure kept showing up. Soon, his paintings were only of this figure. Not a man, not a creature, but an entity of sorts. Humanoid, tall and grey with a gaunt, almost featureless face and a horn protruding from its forehead. Its eyes were vacuous, and often the paintings would depict its hands aflame or smoking. Now, to bring an imaginary character to life through art is one thing, but it's another thing entirely when that character begins talking to you. It told Dylan to do things and to paint certain things, and he would obey. Eventually, he told Blair, the entity told him its name.

In the paranormal field and certainly in demonology, it is believed that names hold power. To know an entity's name is valuable, but to utter it is to invoke that entity in some way. If this thing was sharing its name with Dylan, it was not just a friendly introduction. Perhaps this was the start of an oppression, which can sometimes lead to full-on possession. Either way, it was a red flag.

This went on for some time as the paintings got more and more garish and his substance abuse reached dangerous levels. The walls of his room were covered floor to ceiling with images of the entity. He was surrounded by it, inside and out, as if he had little else to give, save for something intangible—like his soul, perhaps? Surprisingly, though, Dylan decided to reverse trajectory and clean up his life. He tore down most of his paintings and moved out of the hotel. It was reported that he went to rehab and joined the Jehovah's Witnesses, but the damage had been done. He was never quite the same, and a new dark mark was left upon the hotel.

Let's consider the conditions surrounding Dylan's experience: a nefarious history laid the foundation, a tortured yet willing soul helped build the walls, and drugs led to an error in judgment allowing the new tenant to move in—literally, in this case. Dylan's actions and choices permitted something dark to truly take domain in his room.

Remember, possession takes many forms, but it's always about territory. People are territory, but so are locations, and every acquisition is a staging ground for the next attack against a person or a place. The entity may have lost its grip on Dylan, but it was not left empty-handed for its efforts. It had been called into a room, and from that point forward, let any who enter beware. The entity could find Dylan again—time was not an issue. Meanwhile, there would be others to torment. Perhaps even our *SCARED!* crew.

In the seven years that we'd been doing our thing, we'd all grown and changed and learned to look at things much differently. But even though we had more experience and knowledge under our belts, something was holding us back. I, personally, think it was the trap of complacency. We'd become known in the field. We spoke and appeared at conventions and thought (incorrectly!) that we had a firm hand on what was going on in the supernatural realm. Chris had started out as the guy in the middle, open to possibilities, but he'd begun to feel more comfortable in the skeptic camp. He hadn't seen anything during our tenure that convinced him definitively. I was just the opposite; I started out a stout skeptic, but my voracious reading about paranormal topics had forced me to open up more. However, I still doubted people's reports, so after hearing of possible demonic activity at The Grand Midway Hotel, I thought it would make for an interesting documentary but expected little more than just another scary story.

Upon learning that we'd be going to The Grand Midway, I consulted my new mentor. "Hey John, we're going to this place in Windber called The Grand Midway. Know anything about it?"

"When are you going?" he countered.

"Next week, why?"

"I'll see you there, buddy!"

The planets were in alignment for some big guns to help us that first night. We knew John Zaffis would be there, but when we arrived, we discovered that prolific author and investigator, Rosemary Ellen Guiley, had also shown up. The two were old friends and were both on the road for their respective speaking engagements. This was the first time I met Rosemary, and I found her to be friendly and quite knowledgeable about a plethora of topics. We were lucky to have her. Our next surprise guest was demonologist Adam Blai. He was another friend of John and Rosemary's, but more importantly, he also lived at the hotel! Adam worked closely with the Catholic Church on possession cases. He was a photographer with an interest in painting. Whether the planets had actually aligned to allow us such a stellar crew, heaven only knows, but I do believe physical positioning played a part in our investigation.

The hotel had a simple layout. There were three floors connected by the main staircase near the front entrance. The upper two floors had a single hallway with rooms off to each side. The rooms had plaques above the door frames, naming each one for frequent guests or other references. Each room had its own personality and was decorated to portray a unique feeling or concept. The Monkey Room was home to a stuffed monkey prop from *Outbreak*. The Writer's Room was filled with bookshelves and antique typewriters, while another room appeared to be underwater. The Canopy Room had a lattice-wrapped bed sitting catty-cornered between two mirrors, and the Magician's Room could only be accessed through a secret passage behind a bookcase (a surprise that Blair literally finished as we arrived that day).

The unique rooms of The Grand Midway made it a macabre place with a Halloween feel year-round. Dylan's old room was on the third floor at the end of the hallway to the left. Although not the official name, we'd been calling it the "Demon Room." It was actually two smaller rooms, front and rear, making up one space. It was currently unoccupied and empty except for a bed frame with springs and a small couch in the rear room. Even the walls had been stripped down to slats, a skeletal reminder of what once was. All of Dylan's artwork was gone, save for one piece—a lone sentry, seemingly guarding the entryway. The floor-to-ceiling painting occupied a narrow section of wall just left of the door. Someone walking into the room would be unaware of it until they turned around to leave. It was the figure Dylan painted so often.

The eyes were black and lifeless. Its fists were smoking, and its skin seemed to give off heat. Looking at it was uncomfortable, as if gazing too long could cause one to be captured and dragged into the painting. If all the rooms in the hotel were decorated to match their unique energy, then this one was perfectly arranged.

The arrangement was on my mind as I took note of where Adam's room was located. It, too, was on the third floor but on the opposite end and side of the hall. His door was closed, and brilliantly painted on it was an image of the Archangel Michael slaying a dragon. The balance struck me as relevant, but it would be some time before I revisited that concept.

The first night of the investigation would be more scientific. Our psychic, my cousin Lisa Ann, would not arrive until the next day, so this was our chance to let our devices do the brunt of the work. Baseline readings, practical measurements, and experimentation were on the menu. We set up stationary cameras in the rooms we felt had the greatest chance of capturing something. We interviewed Blair, John, Rosemary, and Adam about their past experiences at the hotel. We shot footage of all the rooms on every floor and even explored the basement, which had been dubbed the "Fight Club" due to the Rock 'Em Sock 'Em Robots set at the center of the main chamber. Jason and Greg were assigned to our home base in the Monkey Room to keep watch over the monitors. I conducted several EVP sessions on the upper floors. Chris was stalwart on the camera, capturing every moment attempting to contact whatever unseen personality was in the hotel. We joined Rosemary and Adam in a Geiger Counter experiment; then, we headed up to her room, where John met us for a spirit box session. Brooke spent a lot of time in the Writer's Room, following a feeling that pulled her there.

We had a dream team assembled and went through the steps for a proper investigation, but despite the powerhouse of personalities, there was very little, if any, activity perceived. We gathered at the bar downstairs and discussed the events of the night. Would they work in the documentary? Perhaps we got things on tape that we hadn't yet realized. And if the second night were as quiet as this one was, how would we document such a dry narrative? I had assumed that having so many paranormal veterans present would supercharge the activity, but instead, the night had become a needed reminder of something I always said at events: the supernatural doesn't come on cue.

So we all stood down, some of us retiring to our rooms, some of us relaxing outside. I was about to join Chris outside when Adam approached me.

"I want you to come upstairs with me," he said, somewhat seriously. My guard went up a little.

"What's up?" I replied.

"I want to show you something."

Now, when I tell this story on stage, I usually make a joke about someone connected to the Catholic Church wanting to show me something in private, and it usually gets a chuckle. But in all truthfulness, I was nervous. Not because I thought Adam would do anything to me, but because I could hear the weight in his words. What he was going to show me was deep, possibly dangerous. Concerns aside, I went upstairs with Adam. We went exactly where I knew we would: to the "Demon Room."

Standing at its threshold, Adam explained that he wanted me to be exposed to the energy in the room again so that I would recognize it in the future. This seemed to be a training lesson just for me; it wasn't something the whole team could stumble through. I felt like Luke Skywalker about to enter the Dark Side cave on Dagobah. What lay inside was unknown but surely not friendly.

In we went. I held my EMF meter close to me as I looked around. Earlier, when I'd been on camera, I'd been able to exude a certain confidence, but now that I was here somewhat alone, I felt vulnerable. Adam peered into the upper corners of the room, seeking the familiar "feeling" that seemed to be eluding him.

"It's not here right now. Or if it is, it's hiding from us," he explained.

That wasn't enough for me. All of that lead-up and then nothing? I wasn't expecting to shake hands with the Devil, but I had taken Adam at face value, and I wanted to feel something. My skeptical nature took the podium, and I started asking questions. He had decent enough explanations for this no-show demon, but they only sparked more questions. Remember, I was raised Catholic, so the subject of angels and demons held currency with me. I've always been intrigued by Big Picture questions.

"Okay, follow me on this one," I began, "God's a cool guy, New Testament and all. He's about forgiveness, right?"

Adam nodded, waiting to see where I would go with the thought.

"Can't demons repent? Can't they say, 'Oops, we were wrong to follow Lucifer,' and be forgiven and allowed back into Heaven?"

Adam shook his head. "That's not possible," he said. "We can be forgiven because we are human. Demons were once angels, which means they can see from the beginning of time until the end. They knew the consequences of rebelling, and they did it anyway. For that, they will never be in God's presence again. It's that difference that makes them hate us so much—how we can fall time and time again and still be forgiven, while they cannot. They see it as a grave injustice."

This was a heavy topic, and Adam and I delved into it over the next two hours. We discussed the War in Heaven, the Fall, and other theological concepts. All while in the alleged den of a demon. He told me what Dylan had done and what he had caused. It was an overload of information. I felt a heaviness, not of the oppression in the room, but of the ramifications of what it would mean if these tales from the Bible held any real truth. I returned to my sleeping quarters that night with a lot to think about.

Sadly, we would be losing half of our team the next day as John and Rosemary had lectures to attend. Adam needed to leave town for work as well. Jason and Greg had their other halves demanding they be home, and Blair would be working. The SCARED! Crew would be shaken down to a team of four, three of which made up the Three Pillars, which I find very important when building a team.

Like a baseball team, a paranormal team needs people in different positions. Not everyone can pitch or play shortstop; you need all the bases covered. I had learned that people, while investigating, tended to find what they expect. Meaning if everyone went in believing they were going to find evidence of ghosts, they would find a way to do so, real or not. The reverse is also true. So, to combat this tendency toward expectation bias, we came up with what I called the Three Pillar System. The Three Pillars are: Psychic, Scientist, and Skeptic. Three different viewpoints to make for a more balanced investigation. The evidence collected by such a team would come closer to the truth due to the perceptual tug-of-war among those archetypes. The psychic believes, the skeptic rationalizes, and the scientist measures. We didn't know how well this formula could work until that second night at the hotel.

Night two began with my cousin Lisa Ann's arrival. Whenever she worked with us, we never told her exactly where we'd be investigating. We would just give her a general area and then go collect her, preventing her from researching the location beforehand. We trusted her, but for peer review, such a measure was necessary.

The others had already left, so we launched right into it. We usually began with me performing a scientific sweep while Chris assisted or filmed, then Lisa Ann would do a separate psychic sweep with Greg as her host. She would tell him what she was sensing, and he would ask follow-up questions. Since Greg had gone home, however, we had to alter the roster. In place of Greg, Chris would walk through with Lisa Ann, and I would be behind the camera. It was the first time we three worked together in this manner. Unlike Greg, who was gently inquisitive and amicable, Chris pushed back and challenged Lisa Ann with tough questions, requiring the proof that he and so many others wanted. The two were good friends in everyday life, but it was unknown how their opposing viewpoints would clash on camera. Would Chris's skepticism act as a damper for anything she was trying to connect with? We would soon see.

At first, it went like it always did. Lisa Ann toured the rooms and provided impressions of personalities and past events. Some seemed to be relevant to the hotel itself; others were of a transitory nature. Many seemed to be generic and easily applied to whatever the hotel's history was, a fact that Chris made sure to point out.

"I just say what I'm getting. If it makes sense, that's great, but I'm not going to try and force it to fit," Lisa Ann would always say.

Chris remained unimpressed. I just followed them silently behind the camera.

We wandered about for a while before we got to the third floor. As Lisa Ann examined the rooms, Chris and I kept our eye on the one at the end of the hall. Earlier that day, before Lisa Ann arrived, I had gotten him up to speed with everything Adam and I had talked about the night before. The agenda of demons, Dylan's history, and actions in the hotel—all of it. Chris listened to everything, but in the end, he just shook his head and chuckled, unwilling to accept any of it. I wasn't surprised. Even I was struggling with the information.

As we crept toward the end of the hall, Lisa Ann grew increasingly quiet and less descriptive with her readings. And when we reached the point of only one room remaining, she stopped and looked around, giving the room a half-glance, as if it hardly mattered.

"Okay, guys, was there anywhere else you wanted me to go?"

Chris and I looked at each other and nodded.

"Yeah, into that room there," he said, gesturing to Dylan's room.

Lisa Ann's face stayed poised, but her eyes betrayed her feelings. After a long pause, a sigh escaped her lips as she turned to look at the last room. She clearly didn't want to go in.

"I was hoping you wouldn't ask," she admitted.

We dallied a moment more in the hall and then proceeded inside. I paid special attention to see if I felt anything different than the night before. I can't say that I did, plus, I was emboldened with my friends there.

My musings were interrupted by the shrill whine from the Gauss Master, which Chris was holding. The room no longer had any electrical power running through its gutted walls, and my sweep the night before had revealed no manmade EMF sources. This reading was an anomaly. Lisa Ann was busy looking around the room with her eyes closed as if listening to some unheard audio tour.

The EMF spike was strong and constant. It saturated the whole room, making it hard to pinpoint the origin. Maybe it was the power lines near the street? The phone lines outside the building? The noise from the meter was enough to even break Lisa Ann out of her trance. We went outside to check on the exterior lines passing by Dylan's room, but none of them could explain the readings. Back upstairs we went.

Returning to the room, the meter continued to cry out its discovery. Lisa Ann sat down on the couch and communicated the basics of what she was feeling.

"It's very weird in here," she said. "Almost like a schizophrenic feeling. I think he had visions that tortured him. I'm getting weird things in my head like he would get these crazy thoughts and images."

I asked if this was a residual feeling or someone she was presently speaking with.

"I'm talking to a disturbed young man. He says he's very sad; he didn't mean it, it wasn't his fault," she narrated. "He's young. He suffers some kind of abuse, and he's scared." She went on to describe the boy and some of the things that had happened to him. The story was a familiar one. It sounded like she was describing Dylan.

I couldn't help but think of the conversation I'd had with Adam the night before. Hearing about the hatred demons had for us, how their patience and trickery were tools to lure us into vulnerable positions. All the while, the meter was droning on. Chris and I once again got distracted looking for the source. As we both huddled around the device, I could hear Lisa Ann's voice, but she sounded far away, as if underwater. My focus was fixed solely on the little red needle on the meter display. Maybe that's what it wanted, and yet I could hear her voice tugging at me.

"GUYS! You're not listening to me. He says he wants to know if he can tell you his story. He wants to know if you'll listen."

I snapped out of my haze and back to clarity. He wants to what? Tell me his story? That was a red flag. A red flag accentuated by the meter now blaring out a siren of warning.

You might be wondering why an entity that was willing to communicate concerned me. Great question, but here's the thing: In all the years I had worked with psychics, especially Lisa Ann, never once did a spirit wait for permission to interact and tell their story. Usually, that was their purpose, and they would often overwhelm her with details. Like a dam breaking, the information would wash over her, and it was all she could do to relate the important bits. But here we were, story paused, waiting for us to give the word to continue— never had that happened before. It didn't feel right; it felt sinister. It felt like the first step in a series of mistakes waiting to be made. *Yes, grant me permission. I shall tell you my tale, and you will let me in. The choice is yours. Let me in . . .*

I saw that Chris was also staring at Lisa Ann, probably feeling the same air of warning. What scared me even more than being lured into the mouth of this potentially demonic trap was that Lisa Ann seemed somehow unaware of it. For all her gifts, she couldn't see past one simple deception. *She can't help you. I have her. Just say yes and let me in. It's why you've come. Let me in . . .*

"Come with us, Lisa Ann," Chris said, "we've got to fill you in on some things."

We led her down the hallway and into the bedroom across from Adam's, where we resigned ourselves to telling Lisa Ann all we knew about the case: the history, the reports, and everything about Dylan. For us, this was a major breach in protocol, but the stakes seemed too high to ignore. This wasn't simply about filming a documentary anymore.

Chris and I took turns sharing parts of the tale, and as he spoke, I could see a shift in his demeanor. He stammered a bit, and the pitch of his voice was slightly elevated—he was truly scared. I'd never seen my friend in such a state before, and in turn, it scared me.

We realized the correlation between Dylan's story and specific things Lisa Ann had said about the boy in the room went well beyond generalization and lucky guesses. But Dylan was still alive, so she couldn't be talking to his ghost. Additionally, he stayed at the hotel as an adult, so any residual energy would most likely be that of an adult. Sure, he could have cast off part of his psyche in an attempt to bury old wounds, but more likely, whatever remained in his room was trying to appear docile and meek—a victim, even. By dropping our guard, we would become more vulnerable to attack.

This news angered Lisa Ann. She was a mother, and it was playing up to her maternal nature. But she was also a New Yorker and an Italian. She did NOT like being played with!

"What do you want to do?" I asked.

"I want to get back in there and find out what the hell we're dealing with!"

Hell, indeed. Looking back on that moment, I always find it humorous. We believed an immortal, infernal creature was messing with us, and to talk privately with Lisa Ann, we took her a few doors down, as if that would hide our words and intentions! How ridiculous it sounds now, but at the time, it made us feel better.

Gathering up our resolve and rallying around Lisa Ann and her renewed gusto, we marched back to Dylan's old room. The first thing we noticed was that the energy felt different. Chris maintains he didn't notice anything different, but I remember feeling like all the air had been sucked out of the room. It felt heavy, oppressive, and unwelcoming. The shadows now had daggers pointed at us; the silence, malintent. Lisa Ann looked around and confirmed my fear—something had changed. She said she felt a dark presence that wanted her to fear it. She described seeing images of black, melting people with melting faces. This was terrifying to me because I could not see what she did. All I could do was point the camera and record what she was saying.

"There's an angry spirit here, and he wants to know why I'm here and why it doesn't bother me to be in this room. And I'm telling him I'm not afraid of him," Lisa Ann reported.

Well, you should be. You can't protect them from me.

In the moments that followed, the tension grew. Lisa Ann described the entity as tall and black. It kept trying to stand behind her and threatened her by asking why she wasn't afraid. Each time, she would about-face and declare her lack of fear, which she said pissed it off. And as she continued to rebuke the entity, Chris began to feel chills, an icy finger running up his back, over and over again.

Yes, I can taste the fear from this one. I will have what I want.

The stand-off continued, and the three of us wheeled slowly around the room. I found myself with my back to the wall as I tried to keep them in the frame. Suddenly, I heard a voice behind me, as if someone leaned directly behind my head and whispered harshly. I couldn't make out what was said, but I had to try and explain it. I asked Chris if he had just muttered something. He said no and asked if I'd heard something.

"I don't know," I admitted, "but it was almost behind me." Then I turned to Lisa Ann.

"It's funny," she said, "because I was just thinking, 'My name is . . .' but I didn't hear the name. Because I feel like the guy who was in this room had a name for him—this black entity," Lisa Ann said. "He's waiting for him to come back."

I can wait. Time is on my side. You three will do for now.

I was almost numb from fear at this point. Logic was telling me there was nothing to fear but seeing the expression on my best friend's face as well as hearing the words being spoken by my cousin—I knew they weren't embellishing things for the fun of it; these were people I trusted with my life—we were clearly in the midst of a spiritual battle. I didn't know much about demonic encounters, but I knew the stakes were never small, never inconsequential.

It seemed as if it were finally beginning to affect Lisa Ann too. As she continued to commune with it, she kept moving around and, at one point, jumped back and grabbed Chris for support. She said something grabbed her as she moved towards the couch. If things had escalated to physical barbs, that couldn't be good.

Here we were, in the middle of something one might see in a movie, sans the pyrotechnics. We were in the lair of evil, by choice, mixing it up with something beyond our full comprehension. Was it truly a demon? A personality that has seen God, who was around at the formation of our reality, and chose to ally with Lucifer to participate in the War on Heaven? Could all the tales I'd heard as a child indeed be true? As I wrestled with the theological possibilities, Lisa Ann started mapping out a solution to Blair's infestation issue.

"If they wanted to get rid of him, all they'd have to do is make this room a shrine and bring in statues and deities of different religions . . ." *Shut up! Shut up!* ". . . and they could paint bright colors and suns and positive things . . ." *Shut up!* ". . . but there has to be all different religions. It keeps yelling at me to 'shut up, shut up, shut up' by the way."

Shut up! They don't believe you! Shut up!

At this point, I felt like we'd hit our limit. We weren't *Ghostbusters*; we didn't have proton packs or ghost traps. We weren't exorcists with God on speed dial. We were a group of paranormal investigators who filmed documentaries about our experiences. My camera and EMF detector would not be enough to save our souls. So what was our next move?

On one hand, this was a success—this is what we came here for. We came to experience something supernatural, and so far, we'd been able to check a lot of boxes. Lisa Ann was communicating directly with something. Check. Chris was feeling something touch him. Check. I was hearing voices. Check. Given everything that had already occurred, we felt it was time to wrap things up and leave the room. What else was there? We would soon find out. Could we still be in danger?

I know who you are now.

"You guys need to go out first because I need to make sure he doesn't go with you," Lisa Ann instructed. "I can make sure he doesn't stay with me."

Without any argument, Chris and I backed out of the room. Since I was still filming, I kept her in view as we stepped into the hallway. She stood silently with her eyes closed, meditating or doing whatever a psychic does to ensure she left that room without an attachment. In the past, I had a laissez-faire attitude about attachments—if I ignored them, they would ignore me—but this was an altogether different situation. As the saying goes, there are no atheists in foxholes, and this was one hell of a figurative foxhole.

In conversations with various metaphysical workers I'd met over the years, one common practice was always suggested to ward off negativity—envisioning yourself surrounded in white light. I figured it couldn't hurt to try, and at that moment, any method of protection seemed like a good one. I tilted my head towards Chris, who was standing next to me, and said, "Imagine yourself surrounded in white light."

It was a key moment for both of us. There I was, the scientist, telling the skeptic to employ some hippie, New Age protection method! Chris and I had been friends for many years, and I was already formulating a response to the jab I knew was coming, but instead, my recommendation was met with only a prolonged silence. I eventually turned from the camera to look at my friend. His gaze was transfixed on Lisa Ann, who was still in the room. I even thought I saw his lips moving, perhaps in prayer. The skeptic had experienced something he thought he never would, and so it came to pass that Chris Mancuso and I stood silently in a hallway, envisioning ourselves surrounded in white light. Alert the media!

Shortly after our shared moment, Lisa Ann came striding out of the room.

"We need to find some sage," she said and then took off towards the stairs.

Chris and I followed on her heels, eager to get as far away from that room as possible. As we reached the second level, our case manager, the only other human in the hotel at the time, rushed up to us.

"Guys, what happened? I kept hearing things down here at home base."

We didn't answer. We couldn't. The three of us were, for lack of a better term, shell-shocked. We were having a hard time putting into words what had just occurred. It was too fresh, and we still had to process it all.

The next few minutes were a rush of action as Lisa Ann was instructed by her spirit guides where to find some sage (behind the bar on the first floor). We all went outside, and she went to her car to get her rosary beads and Mother Mary medallion. Then came the smudging. With no objection and with some measure of relief, I let Lisa Ann use the sage to cleanse me of any residual negative energy. She did the same for the others and herself.

Chris and I sat on the train tracks in front of the hotel, rocking back and forth. He smoked a cigarette while I stared at my hands and tried to make sense of what had just happened. We felt better being outside, but the window at the top left of the hotel was Dylan's room, and it felt as if it were staring down at us, watching, waiting. Our case manager excitedly listened to Lisa Ann as she related some of what went on up there. She then told us she wanted to conduct an EVP session in Dylan's room.

"Not a chance!" I countered. "You are not going up to that room!"

She argued, but Chris and I maintained it was not a good idea. This was no longer a fun, "what if" kind of situation. It was a hot zone that needed to be treated as such. We didn't want her to put herself in danger for curiosity's sake. We didn't want her to put us in danger either. There were still so many unknown variables. We barely understood the experience ourselves, let alone how we'd explain it to others.

I always marvel at the types of things people desire to experience. At conventions, I often hear tales of paranormal occurrences to which listeners respond, "I want to see that for myself!" Especially when it comes to the demonic. Why on Earth would you want to experience that? Expressing envy over a reported demonic encounter seems akin to standing on a street corner, hoping to see someone get hit by a truck or perhaps even get hit yourself. Just to see what it's like!

What we witnessed at The Grand Midway didn't feel good. What made it worse was that we had to go back inside and spend the night, knowing what was in there with us. I was loath to close my eyes and sleep. It felt like a vulnerability. Do demons sleep?

When we first arrived, we had all chosen rooms to sleep in. I had selected the Writer's Room, directly below the "Demon Room." Call it superstition, but something made me switch rooms that first night, and I relocated down the hall to the Kerouac Room—bookshelves and typewriters were replaced by cameras, maps, and a poster of two young women kissing. I slept comfortably there the first night. Now I was doubly relieved I had switched rooms, even though, like when we took Lisa Ann down the hall, I don't know what the distance of a few hundred feet would accomplish against a minion of Hell. But sleep was the furthest thing from our minds. Even though it was never expressed verbally, none of us wanted to be alone. We continued to talk as we slowly reentered the hotel, all the while armoring ourselves for the challenge of sleeping in a demon-infested building. It wasn't until the light of the sun crept into my window that the others left my room to go to theirs.

Those few hours of sleep were restless ones, haunted by the events of the night before. My body felt sore as if I had just run a marathon with an elephant strapped to my back. All my fears and insecurities had been probed in the murky moments that preceded my return to consciousness. The morning was a sunny one, in direct contrast to my mood.

I had slept with my door wide open since it made me feel less alone. The symbol of an open door had so many connotations in this situation, but I only wanted to feel closer to my friends, whose nearby rooms also had open doors.

I heard shuffling in the corridor. I coughed loudly to indicate I was awake. A curly-haired silhouette peeked around my door frame—our case manager. An early riser by nature, she was awake well before I was and had been padding around the hallway for a little while. I could also hear activity echoing from downstairs—welcomed signs of life.

"How did you sleep?" she asked.

"Not well. I had a hard time getting all the way asleep."

"Well, Chris is missing," she stated matter-of-factly.

"What!" I snapped back.

That was not the piece of news I was expecting so early in the morning. Missing? How so? I was having a hard time sorting through the cobwebs in my mind to really understand what she was telling me. As I'd tossed and turned, she had checked in on each of us and found our lead investigator not in his room.

My best friend was a curious specimen. He had numerous redeeming qualities as well as a few strange ones, which made him fun to be around, but he also baffled us most of the time. In a 33-room hotel (minus the ones already occupied, of course), he'd had many options but had nevertheless chosen the Monkey Room, whose main feature was a taxidermal monkey sitting in a wheelchair—no couch, no bed, and a laminate floor. It looked like the lobby of some 70's era city flophouse. Other rooms offered comfortable beds and better themes, but no, he wanted to room with the prop from *Outbreak*. And now he was nowhere to be found.

"Maybe he's outside having his morning smoke," I suggested.

"I checked there. I checked all the other empty rooms, and he's not in any of them. Blair hasn't seen him either," she answered.

Blair worked the late-night shift at a bar in town and had not been around for our encounter. He returned home shortly after we'd all turned in. Presently, I could hear his voice coming from somewhere in the hotel. I could also hear my cousin. The only one not accounted for was Chris. Had the demon gotten him?

The search was short but tense as we overturned each room, looking for our lead investigator. This was before everyone had a cell phone strapped to them at all times, so we had to actually look with our own eyes. My task was to check the third floor, and as I approached the last room on the left, I paused to stare at it. The morning sun made everything feel more cheerful as if the events of the previous night had never happened—though I knew they had. I didn't want to forget that. Despite my ever-present skepticism, I did not want to let my guard down, just in case. But I had to check the room to be sure Chris was not in there. I considered myself a scientist. Fear would not dictate my actions.

Slowly I made my way across the hall into the "Demon Room." I thought once again of my conversation with Adam, as well as the previous night's encounter. I allowed myself to try and feel what was here, but I felt nothing. The bare, exposed-slat walls almost seemed comforting with the early morning sun shining in on them. I looked around briefly and projected my intent.

I don't know if you're still here, but you are not allowed to follow me back out, I thought. *I'm just looking for my friend. You're not allowed to touch him either.*

The room was still and quiet, showing no signs of battle or conflict. The garish form in the painting beside the door looked on silently. If it had any power of its own, it was like a gargoyle, roaming free at night while staying dormant during the day. Regardless, I wasn't going to test that theory, and after confirming Chris wasn't in there, I hurried back downstairs.

It turns out Chris had gotten cold on the floor of the Monkey Room and found his way past the bookshelf into the secret Magic Room behind it. With the hidden door closed, we had no idea where he had gone until he emerged from his literary crypt.

The rest of the morning went well as we packed up, said goodbye to Blair, and headed back east towards home. As the miles added up, we assumed the story had ended. But remember my checklist of experiences as we exited the "Demon Room?" Another discovery was yet to be made, and we were still in danger.

***

Back home, life went on as usual over the next few weeks. Footage from the weekend was loaded onto the computer, and we prepped the next shoot as we began editing the latest documentary. Then one night, Chris called me on the phone with disbelief in his voice.

"Dude, I, I don't know what to say. You've got to hear this. I've been going over the footage from this scene, and I've played it at least a hundred times, no joke, and I might be going crazy," he stammered.

He'd been editing the scene of us standing in the hallway imagining ourselves in white light. It was a humorous scene that we'd flagged to talk about in the interviews. We found the exercise absurd, but thankfully we'd done it because we'd caught an EVP right on the camera audio!

I went over to his house that night, and we sat by the computer listening to the clip another hundred times, unable to comprehend what we heard. The scene happened exactly as we remembered, save for one addition—voices that were not our own. The camera was pointed at Lisa Ann as she was preparing to back out of the room. Off-camera, you hear my voice softly telling Chris to imagine himself surrounded in white light. Some ten seconds later, we heard the following:

"Can you break out of the circle? The circle of fire?" came the voice.

"Die," came the second one.

We listened to it again and again. Most captured EVPs are a word or a short phrase. This was a full sentence—a query, followed by a response! But what did it mean? What circle? And it wanted us to die? The latter word was hissed as a chilling command as if its utterance alone would deliver the desired result. What made the whole thing even more disturbing was the voice itself. It sounded like Blair.

We were familiar with the concept that spirits can mimic voices. A voice was just a sound wave at a certain frequency, so by matching it, a spirit could sound like anyone, but especially someone they'd observed before, like the owner of the hotel. We also confirmed that Blair had been at work the entire time we were investigating, so we know it wasn't him. The tale was getting weirder and weirder.

We moved on to the meaning of the EVP. What was it trying to tell us, beyond the threat of shuffling us loose the mortal coil? The circle of fire—what was that? Having no idea, we turned to John and Adam, both demonologists. In his customary way, John contemplated the issue while offering little upfront advice, allowing us space to first draw our own conclusions. On the other hand, Adam was able to give some more background on the "Demon Room" and its occupant. His room was at the other end of the floor, on the opposite side of the hall, as far away as he could get while still on the same level. Being a man of God who worked closely with the Catholic Church, Adam had blessed the hotel several times, as well as many of its rooms, save for that one. That room he was asked to leave alone by Blair.

A brief word about Blair and his upbringing. As I mentioned, he came from a family of morticians, so the macabre was always a part of his world, and he embraced it. He decorated every inch of the hotel, and his sensibilities gave it an *Addams Family* meets *The Munsters* vibe. It was a Halloween Land, where even Jack Skellington would feel at home. So, the concept of a demon, or at the very least a malevolent spirit, living in his hotel was something he did not fear. If anything, it added to the decor. On top of that, he had an ironic "live and let live" attitude towards it. "Leave it alone, and it'll leave me alone," he'd say.

Because of that decree, Adam did as he was asked and never blessed that particular room. However, because the rest of the hotel had been blessed, he suggested the demon saw the blessing as fire. The circle of fire. Something harmful that it couldn't cross. We could cross it, though, and that made the demon want to kill us. *Die!* It was aware of us, and it wanted us dead. Not the enemy one wanted to have. This experience colored my existence over the next two years.

My natural cynicism was exacerbated by the thought that the world was being invaded room-by-room, person-by-person by demons. I would see on the news how the world was getting closer to chaos every day. Politics, the economy, the environment, people in general—it all seemed to be going to hell, and there was nothing I could do about it. It's a horrible way to live, feeling helpless as I did during those years. My visit to The Grand Midway caused echoes in my life that continue to ring out to this day. This tale was not yet done.

As fate would have it, I found myself inside The Grand Midway again, this time with John Zaffis as we were filming an episode of *Haunted Collector*. For a show about haunted items and their effect on people, the hotel delivered an interesting tale regarding the miners who had stayed there in the past. While the others on the cast were excited to explore this new location, I was dour. If you get a chance to see the episode in reruns, watch the beginning section, where we offer any background of the case to John. Usually, we'd all serve up a factoid or two, and then John would make the marching orders. This time, Aimee, Chris Zaffis, Jason, and Jesslyn all cheerfully piped in with their bits while I sat there silently, a particular look on my face. I knew what was in there. I knew what awaited us on the third floor. Like Gandalf, when the Fellowship decided to go through Moria, I secretly winced and prepared myself for battle.

A couple of years had passed, and I wondered how the demon perceived time. Was it aware I had returned? Would it recognize me? I recalled that morning years ago when our *SCARED!* crew had been prepping to leave the hotel. By chance, the painter Dylan heard we were there and came down over to see what was happening. He appeared an emaciated, broken man, doing his best to walk the narrow line. I'd always heard that once possessed, even if you broke free, you'd always have to be on guard. You would forever be at risk. So it seemed, for this tortured soul. He spoke mostly to Blair, but as Chris and I packed the car, he asked if we had pictures of his paintings. He wanted to see them one more time, like Bilbo asking Frodo to see the One Ring. You could hear the temptation and pull in his voice. The Thing in the room was calling him even then. We told him we didn't have any, even though we did. It would've been cruel to expose him to his addiction. Furthermore, given what we'd just experienced, we thought it best not to interact with him too much.

So there I was once again, on the front porch of the hotel, watching the film crew go in and out, setting up lights and cameras in preparation for the shoot. It was a cold, overcast morning that reflected my mood. I was happy to be working on the show and happy to see Blair again but concerned about what might happen. Blair and I had become friends over the years, and Chris and I would always try to visit him during our October lecture circuit. We knew better than to mess with the room, or its occupant, so we kept the visits brief and rarely went near it. Speaking of Chris, he would soon be arriving to be interviewed as a witness for the show. I pitched the hotel to the producers and told them everything we'd experienced there, offering up our documentary as a reference. I insisted that one of the interviews be with my friend.

We had filmed the introduction and walkthrough segments, and it was time to get to the preliminary investigation.

"Okay, Chris (Zaffis) and Brian, why don't you guys go check out the basement. Jason and Jesslyn, I want you to go to the third floor," John ordered.

I shivered. Getting sent to a basement was par for the course, but what bothered me was Jason and Jesslyn being exposed to the danger on the third floor. I was confident that Jason could handle himself if push came to shove, but I was worried that Jesslyn's enthusiasm might put them at risk. She sometimes reminded me of our case manager on *SCARED!*, more focused on the hunt than the consequences, so intent on proving herself that she would ignore the warning signs. This could go south fairly quickly.

Later that night, I joined Chris Mancuso at the Holiday Inn in town to brief him on what had happened earlier that day. While the investigation had gone routinely for Jason and Jesslyn, something did happen that justified my worry. John often liked to do EVP sessions during the first half of a case, and this one was no different. As we were hanging around outside in between filming segments, I asked him how it went. He replied that it went fine, that there were a couple of EVPs of note. Curious, I asked to hear them—what I heard on John's recorder took me back years to that night in the hallway outside Dylan's room.

It should be noted that as the years pass since this second trip to the hotel, some of the details fade. I don't remember the exact phrase of this second EVP recording nor the response. It has since disappeared from John's device. But I do remember what it sounded like or, rather, who it sounded like. Once again, we had another EVP in Blair's voice.

"No way!" Chris said in shock.

"That's not all," I reported. "John conducted his session on the second floor. The second floor, not the third!"

Our landmark EVP had been collected outside Dylan's room—the circle of fire allegedly was in place, making sure the demon stayed in there. But if the same entity was now doling out verbiage one floor down, its territory must have expanded to other rooms and floors—and very possibly people. How many had been affected in the two years since our interaction? Could the circle of fire have been broken?

I'd asked John if there was something we should be worried about or if we could do anything to fix it. "Eh, it'll be fine," he dismissed. *Fine! It'll be fine?* John's words, instead of comforting me, only served to alarm me. He was a veteran in the field and, furthermore, a demonologist. In this moment, though, his judgment seemed skewed, compromised even. Could John Zaffis have been affected by the demon?

As I was relating this all to Chris, he puffed calmly on his cigarette. Then I noticed what he was wearing around his neck, and suddenly the whole situation snapped into focus. On our lecture tour, Chris would say to audiences that our experiences at The Grand Midway taught us real evil existed. It was out there, and it posed a danger to all of us. But there was a balance in the Universe, right? If there was Evil, there was Good to oppose it, and you had to choose a side. The silver cross around his neck boldly declared his side.

We both took a moment to reflect on the past. Specifically, the message contained within the now-infamous EVP. *Can you break out of the circle; the circle of fire . . . Die!* All this time, we had assumed the communication was directed at us. Of course, it was for us, we'd figured, who else would it be for? Our egos had gotten in the way. The capture was an amazing one, yes, but our presence for it was superfluous. We just happened to be present for an exchange between two entities. Two!

Imagine the exchange between a prisoner and a guard.

"How do you like your cell, convict?" says the guard.

"Screw you, pig," replies the prisoner.

Apply that to the EVP. Something queried if the entity could leave the room, the circle of fire. Since it could not, it prompted an angry response: *Die!* Neither part of the exchange was meant for us. But this new realization made me feel immeasurably better. For the past two years, I had felt a growing darkness was taking hold across the world, and there was little we could do about it. Beyond the church and the demonologists and people in that category, the average paranormal investigator like me had no chance against such evil. We weren't just losing the battle; we weren't even in the fight. But I had forgotten about balance. I'd focused on the dark side only. If there are demons out there, then there are also angels. If there was a demon trapped in Dylan's old room, then perhaps, there was an angel keeping watch over him. It made me think again of the painting on Adam's door, the one of the Archangel Michael slaying a dragon. Maybe Michael wasn't there, but it sounded like someone was.

John knew that. He was content to let the powers that be wheel around each other and fight their own battles. I felt much better. The sun would come up again in the morning. It would dawn on a world where there was hope and those striving to make things better. It wasn't our responsibility to fight the good fight all by ourselves. Yes, demons existed, but we had some heavy hitters on our side as well. It took an intense experience and several years of reflection to realize that.

I'm often asked what my scariest experience has been. My time at The Grand Midway is always the answer. It was quite a learning experience, and I wouldn't change a thing. It was also an experience that linked me to the place in a way I could never have imagined. Since then, I've been back there for many fun and creative events. I've spoken at DraculaCon. Chris and I locked ourselves in the hotel for a week for what we called "Writer's Jail." We played undead versions of those writers in Blair's satire film, *Zombie Dream*. We even based an entire expansion of our paranormal card game (The Three Pillars) on The Grand Midway. In 2016, I was part of the team that set a Guinness World Record for painting the World's Largest Ouija Board on the hotel's roof.

Dylan's room has long been cleared. I've been in it and felt nothing. No fear, no worry. Nevertheless, I'm pretty sure more adventures await me in Windber, and I can't wait to discover what they are.

7

My Tech Guy

've never been a fan of the expression "Everything happens for a reason." It feels like a lazy acceptance of things beyond one's control. I've spent most of my adult life trying to carve out an existence of my own choosing, so to think that I might contradict some inevitable grand plan was always problematic to me. Free Will and all, right? My life is my own.

Comedian Kyle Kinane does a bit of stand-up that I absolutely love on the topic. He says that "said reason" for which things happen is usually science. Yes, I agree with that generalization! Actions have consequences. We make choices and then bear out the results of those choices. So, by that logic, the "reason" later perceived as pre-determined is, in truth, nothing more than the evolution of the original choice. My stomach hurts because I ate bad seafood earlier in the day. I got the promotion because I spent months working hard and making sure my superiors were aware of it. Both are examples of how "Everything happens for a reason" is otherwise known as cause and effect. Kinane also points out how those confronted with the illogic of their statement often double down on the sentiment with, "Well, the Lord works in mysterious ways . . ."

Mysterious ways indeed! I rage against the concept! Well, I did.. .

These days I am a little more open to the possibility of a great plan. I mean, the fortune teller did tell me I'd end up on TV, right? Perhaps she got a glimpse at the cosmic blueprints of my life. If there was any string of events that might make me believe in such a concept, it was the one leading up to me becoming "Brian, my tech guy" on *Haunted Collector.*

***

When people ask how I got involved with John Zaffis, I always reply, "You can't be seriously involved in the paranormal for an extended amount of time and not run into John Zaffis." Perhaps that's why they call him the Godfather; if you're doing business in his territory, you have to meet with the top dog. My first interaction with the man was at Phenomenology 101, a convention in Gettysburg, PA. It would eventually become the nation's biggest annual para family reunion, but it was a big question mark that first year, especially for Chris Mancuso and me. *SCARED!* was finally getting established, our names were becoming known, and we wanted to make a good impression, show up strong. That was always our motto: "Show up strong."

I was excited to discover that John would be one of the guests at the event. I had even written him on MySpace (remember MySpace?), telling him I would love to pick his brain if he had time. He responded amicably, as is his way, and I looked forward to learning a few things from him if I could.

"He's one of the bigwigs," I said to Chris as we drove. "He's worked on a ton of cases over the years. There's a lot we can learn from him."

The event was held at the Eisenhower Hotel and Convention Center. Situated on a hill, the complex had multiple levels and several ground floors. As our van slowed near what appeared to be the front entrance, I prepared to hop out and check us in. That's when I noticed him, just inside the doorway—John Zaffis! He was standing at a counter, nodding to a woman on the other side.

"Chris, look! There he is!"

"Yeah," Chris said, "but look at that sign. Registration is up the hill."

We noticed through the windshield that a crowd of people in mostly black shirts had gathered near a larger entrance, several hundred yards away. That was the place we needed to be. So we drove up the hill and parked along the curb.

The lobby was alive with the hustle and commotion of the event's early stages. People were greeting each other, hugging, and laughing.

Crates and suitcases were being rolled down hallways towards rooms. Wristbands were being affixed, and schedules perused. And at the check-in desk was John Zaffis.

"What? How did he get here so fast?" Chris exclaimed. It seemed physically impossible for the man to have walked the great distance from the bottom of the hill, gotten to the front of the line, and checked in before we were able to get there. Yet, amazingly, there he was. That was our first impression of the man. As the weekend progressed, he would continue to baffle us with his ability to appear and disappear seemingly at will.

Our first encounter with him came one night as everyone was relaxing and hanging out. I found Chris outside having a cigarette with some new friends. We were sharing a few laughs and anecdotes when out walked the Godfather of the Paranormal. The group welcomed him warmly. It was a party night, so many of us had had a drink or two—Chris several more. He was rambunctious, to say the least, and shocked everyone by bluntly asking the question we'd been considering all weekend.

"Hey Zaffis," he began, slurring his speech, "I just gotta know: how many of you are there?"

I was mortified. The others chuckled.

John stood expressionless. "How do you mean?" he finally replied.

"I mean, everywhere we go, there you are. We see you down one hallway, then walk in a different direction and see you there. We see you everywhere!" Chris accented his points with exaggerated arm movements as John tried to follow the stream of words.

"What? You're saying you had a dream about me?" John pushed.

Chris's eyes widened, and he began to stammer. "No, no, no—I mean, you seem to be everywhere. You're like Jason Voorhies, and we're in the forest running from you, but then you pop up in front of us!" Chris mimed each motion as he spoke it, much to my chagrin. I could see our paranormal career ending that night.

"Wait, let me get this straight—you had a dream about me and Jason Hawes running around in a forest?" John did not seem amused. The rest of the crowd held their breath.

"No, wait, Zaffis, I meant that you make . . ."

"I'm naked in the forest with Jason?"

Everyone, save for me, giggled at that image. John looked around as if to say, can you believe this guy? He looked at me and my astonished expression, and I think that's what broke him. Laughter erupted from the old man, and the rest of the group joined in. Chris looked shocked, as if he still didn't understand what was happening. It took me a second to snap out of it as well before realizing the old man was having some fun at our expense. That was our next impression of him. John Zaffis liked to joke around. The Godfather had a sense of humor. We learned a lot more about the man from that point forward—in ways we'd never imagined we would.

***

The traffic heading north on I-95 was lighter than usual as Chris and I sped towards Stratford, CT. A couple of years had passed since we'd met John in Gettysburg, and for the past few months, we'd been shooting a documentary about his life. We were on our way to show him the final cut. It was one of the most fun shoots we'd ever been a part of as we inserted ourselves into the daily life of John Zaffis. We learned a lot about the paranormal, as well as the man himself. Out of it, he gained a nickname (Ziggity), and we learned how to speak Ziggity—that is, we became very familiar with his mannerisms and modes of communication.

When we first got tapped to work on the project, we had no idea how we would accomplish any of it. It was one thing to produce episodes of *SCARED!*, where no one was waiting on its delivery, and we had no one to please but ourselves. But this? We were both honored and terrified to work on the story of this man's life.

I was still working at the ad agency when we accepted the offer. Last-minute late nights and weekend work were common occurrences. We had said yes at the top of the year, with a hard deadline of Labor Day weekend. The plan was to premiere the film at Dragon Con in Atlanta before an audience of thousands. I had attended that convention for many years at that point, and for humble documentarians like us, it was considered the big time. One of the biggest pop culture fandom conventions around, it featured programming tracks focused on many interests. There was a *Star Trek* track, an Anime track, a Comic Book track, just to name a few—and this year would see the introduction of the Paranormal track. The pressure was definitely on us to produce a quality documentary.

Chris and I had several meetings in my apartment where we planned out how the shoots could go. We fitted bits in here and there around our daily lives and my time-encompassing job. The first step was to interview John and see what we could glean from that. The day was pure gold. To say John Zaffis is loquacious is an understatement. Even the simplest questions prompt lengthy answers filled with interesting facts and side notes. He even seeds his own follow-up questions, which he then answers within the same stream of consciousness. Getting that footage back to the editing room had us buzzing with excitement as we saw many ways we could build the narrative. The interview itself clocked in at just under two hours, so for a 90-minute documentary, we had a lot to work with. We just had to find a way to schedule and shoot the other parts we wanted to include. I would soon learn the Universe had already planned for that.

As our paranormal profile in the field grew, we got offered more and more interesting projects. But thus far, TV had never knocked on our door. Then one day at work, I got an email from a colleague informing me that a television show had tapped her group to talk about a particular haunt nearby, but none of them could make the shoot. She asked if I would be interested in filling in for them. It was an exciting prospect, but the catch was that it had to happen that day. I'd have to rush straight home from work, change clothes, and then head into Jersey, hoping all the while that traffic cooperated. It would be tight. I immediately called Chris and relayed the info. He said he'd be standing by when I got home, ready to go.

If only I were able to leave work early. I was figuring out the logistics in my head when my work phone rang, summoning me to Human Resources. Short version: I was downsized that afternoon, with no avenue to save my job. As I sat on the express bus headed home, with a box of my knick-knacks on my lap, I felt the sort of excited numbness that comes with the early stages of shock. The first thing I did when I stepped through my front door was call Chris.

"What are you doing home so early?" he asked.

"I lost my job today."

"What! Holy shit, dude, are you serious?"

"Yes. So we're going to have a lot more time to shoot this documentary."

The Universe had cleared the boards for me to work on the story of John Zaffis's life—on the very day that I would make my first actual TV appearance on a paranormal show. That segment from

Most Terrifying Places in America pops up from time to time as a residual haunt of that day.

We completed the film, and the premiere of *John Zaffis: The World Within* went on as planned. From that point forward, our names were linked to John's.

***

The following year found me still without a steady job, leaving me open to part two of the Universe's plan: *Haunted Collector.*

John had been working with a production company to make the show (with the working title *Paranormal Pickers*). It was to be a family affair, featuring John, his wife, and their children. The show was still in development, but the SyFy Channel (then, still SciFi) had picked it up. It would air in the coveted Wednesday 9 PM slot, domain of the trailblazer, *Ghost Hunters.* And the network was looking to add a cast member who specialized in equipment—a tech guy. I'm not sure how many people were considered before me, but I eventually got the call from John.

"You're not doing anything right now, right? Why don't you come on the show?" he proposed. For me, there wasn't even a need to deliberate—I wanted in! In addition to me, they also were adding long-time Paranormal Research Society of New England (PRSNE) team member, Beth Ezzo, with whom I'd just worked with while filming John's documentary.

The following weeks proved stressful as the inner workings of network television pushed and pulled on my emotions. Why, you might ask? Because I'd signed away my rights to be on the show! As I've already said, our profile was growing, and in January 2011, we were offered a contract by a production company looking to make a show about urban exploration. Having seen *SCARED!*, they thought they could make us the next bad boy TV explorers. There was a huge industry expo at the end of the month—ideas were pitched, shows were sold, and marching orders were handed out for the next season of programming. We expected to be among those orders, but it was not to be. By February, our television dream was already dead in the water. Worse, even though this production company wasn't going to do anything with us, we'd signed a year-long option agreement, meaning that we couldn't work with anyone but them for the next year. It seemed like no big deal until John invited me onto his show the very next month. (A word of caution for all who have been or will be approached by production companies offering you the next big show—be careful what you sign. If a prospective project is not snapped up right away, most often, it is abandoned as producers search for something or someone else. It's a dog-eat-dog business for sure.) Like a child of divorcing parents, I was caught in a custody battle. SyFy wanted me on the show, but the other production company "wasn't in the practice of letting their talent out of their contracts." It was a spiteful situation, in my opinion. They didn't want to use me for any of their projects, but they also didn't want me to get cast on any competing programs. Such is the business, I've learned.

Each day came with flip-flopping news reports. On Monday, everything was fine, and I'd be added to the cast, but on Tuesday, the original production company refused to allow it. Wednesday came with a call from John, telling me the president of SyFy was going to bat for me. Thursday arrived with the news that nothing could be done, and they were going to look for my replacement. These were how my weeks went for at least a month.

On one of those nail-in-coffin days, I felt so sad over the situation that I spitefully began editing a new *SCARED!* project, which would become *The Paranormal Investigator's Casebook, Vol. 2.* It's scary how much work I've done over the years motivated by spite, thinking I didn't need anyone else and that I'd do just fine on my own. Yeah, right. That night, I watched *What Dreams May Come,* starring Robin Williams, for the first time. It was not the sort of movie that would cheer me up, but I was in the right mind space to understand it. If I'd seen it when it first came out, that would not have been the case. But spending time in the paranormal had prepared me for the movie's hopeful message. I needed many tissues that night as I wept for the characters on screen and mourned the loss of my chance to go on the road with John. Then, suddenly, it was all okay.

Like a morning of sunshine after a night of storms, I was in Connecticut on the set of the show. I would later find out that an arrangement had been made between the two production companies. It turns out that the company I had signed the agreement with received a sum of money greater than what I made for all of season one on the show, releasing me from my contract. Now that's a way to make a living. Money for nothing, indeed!

It could be said that my work in the field landed me the role and that I deserved it. It could also be said that I just got lucky. Believe me; I've heard it all over the years. The whispered opinions that others should have been cast in my place or that I somehow undeservingly "cut in line." Regardless, it happened. Was it destiny or just a coincidental arrangement of events? Did all those things happen for a reason? Meeting John, working on his documentary, me losing my job when I did—was it all part of a grand plan? If so, did my actions help foster it along or hinder the process? Does my examination of it and the allowance of the possibility earn me any points in the grand scheme of things?

Honestly, I couldn't say. It's entirely possible that I am still in the midst of this story and won't be able to "comprehend and understand" (a binary Ziggityism) it all until the very end. But looking at it from this point on the timeline, it does seem like something was orchestrating the actions and circumstances that landed me where I am now.

So, does everything happen for a reason? I still don't know, but I'm definitely more open to the possibility.

8

You Will Learn

In the paranormal field, I label myself the scientist. I observe, gather data, and then, hypothesize based on what I have in front of me. I've never been one to try and force what I see into a presupposed belief.

I've gone through many phases in my search for answers: believer, skeptic, and my current phase as a skeptical believer. I know that paranormal phenomena exist; I just don't always trust the people who report them. An example that I use all the time goes like this: I know that kangaroos exist, but if you told me you saw one outside my house, I would be highly skeptical of your report. Is it possible? Yes, but highly unlikely. So, you see, it's not that I don't believe in the marsupial or your power of observation; I just know there is probably a more rational explanation.

When I was a part of *SCARED!,* Chris and I agreed that the best format for a paranormal team was the Three Pillar System I introduced in chapter six. As a quick review, the three pillars are psychic, scientist, and skeptic. Three different viewpoints allow for a more well-rounded investigation. It was a system of checks and balances, a tug-of-war almost. We believed whatever was gathered and averaged between the lenses of those three perspectives would be closest to the actual truth. I was the scientist. I wasn't looking to prove or disprove the paranormal. I was looking to measure it, quantify it, and establish norms and guidelines so that others could follow along.

Even though I'd spent my time in the skeptic's camp, I really enjoyed the middleman role of the scientist. It freed me from all the manifestos and declarations one made when choosing a side. The scientist still operates on faith, however—faith in the data placed before him. We trust in those enlightened philosophers and researchers who inform us about the world around us, and we take it on faith that they are correct. Until they are not. Take a glance back through the history of our species. There was a time when we knew that the Earth was flat. There was a time when we knew that all other heavenly bodies orbited the Earth. We once knew that gnomes or other tiny creatures were to blame for the maladies we experienced. To quote the movie *Men in Black*, "Imagine what you'll know tomorrow."

We place our belief in what we think we know until it is disproven and another explanation takes its place. The facts, in black and white, will guide the way. That is the job of the scientist, to outline those facts, which in turn fuel belief. It allows for a more flexible mindset, as new information alters one's perspective.

To paraphrase another movie, *Dogma* by director Kevin Smith, 'belief is a hard thing to change.' To hold a belief is to put all your chips on a number and then stand by it 'til the bitter end, no matter what alternatives are presented. Beliefs are rigid, nonnegotiable. Just think how many people have died for their beliefs. It's better to have ideas. Ideas are flexible, changeable, adaptable in the wake of new information.

The scientist can modify what they put forth because their ideas are formed by the changing data at hand. Newton established a universe of constant gravity until Einstein came along and showed it was variable depending on where in the universe you were. Both men are considered geniuses, and both helped us get where we are now. It's also fair to say that both were considered crazy or subversive in their own time. But that's just another hiccup of human nature—our inability to react well to big changes. I'm a case in point. The stories in this book and the lessons I seek to impart took years for me to accept. I've often been told that I can be quite stubborn, to which I would reply, "No, I'm not!" I'm no stranger to situational sarcasm.

Throughout my years of discovery and growth in the paranormal field, I've had several of what I call *Oh, Shit!* moments. They were occurrences and concepts that shook the foundation of what I thought to be true at the time. For instance, when I first discovered what electronic voice phenomena (EVP) was, it took me some time to digest. *What—are you kidding me? You can capture ghostly voices on tape?!*

Oh, shit! Later, when I found out about real-time methods of instrumental trans communication (ITC), I was again blown away.

I've always compared the assimilation of paranormal theory to the stages of loss. In their own time, each person must go through the phases—denial, anger, bargaining, and finally acceptance. We grieve the loss of our prior worldview, which can be jarring for most. I know it was for me.

I had one of my most poignant *Oh, Shit!* moments at a place called The Seven Sisters Inn in Ocala, FL. To be honest, when it comes to events, sometimes one reverts to autopilot. The supernatural is not a Broadway show where all the action is choreographed and executed to the minute, although there is often a lot of proverbial singing and dancing. At an event, I'm an entertainer as well as a lecturer, and when things just aren't happening, it's my job to make sure the people are having a good time. That can be quite the challenge when trying to deliver a profound, even life-changing, experience. So I do the best I can.

Each room in the bed and breakfast was decorated in the style of a specific city. I was staying in the Cairo room, which, as one might imagine, was filled with sarcophagi, statues of Egyptian deities, and other such curiosities. All of its lavishness truly made me feel like a pharaoh. It was also among the rooms being investigated that night.

Half a dozen people sat quietly on the floor, peering at the shadows poised in the corners of the room. I stood before them at the end of the bed and related the basics of conducting a proper EVP session. Once the rules were established, we got underway. We asked our questions, paused for responses, and then, after everyone got to participate, I shut off the recorder so we could listen back.

When it comes to EVP sessions, people often assume that the responses must coincide with the questions asked. If you ask how old the entity is, you hope to get a numerical response. If you ask if they're a man or woman, you listen for the answer and judge the pitch if one does come across. Here's the catch, though: No covenant has ever been made with the spirit world about the rules and regulations of making contact. The parameters we give for conducting sessions are a rough series of guesses we've made over the years associated with success levels. To assume otherwise is folly. That being said, we still try.

I pressed play on the recorder. We listened intently to the low hiss of the room tone, waiting to decipher any errant noise. Some questions seemed to garner responses. Faint, wispy breaths that made us wonder if we'd made contact. While not an official textbook chart, there is a Class Rating System investigators use to describe the clarity of an EVP, ranging from A to C, with Class A being the most clear and decipherable. The sounds we heard fell into the B and C categories, which means they were subject to debate. Despite what many television shows depict, not all EVPs can be Class A. If that were indeed the norm, then capturing one wouldn't be a phenomenon, would it? It would be just another day at the office.

During the recording, someone had a phone app running, one that would speak words allegedly prompted by a flux in electromagnetic energy. For much of the recording, those words were the clearest non-human responses we got. That is, until we got the Class A we had been hoping for. It delivered a message whose meaning wouldn't be clear until much later.

"Who's here with us?" played the recorded voice of the attendee.

"SISTER" chimed in the app.

"Tag," I noted, "that was the app."

Just then, another voice came across. It was low and gravelly, like that of an older man. I'm usually not one to try and assign gender or age to a disembodied voice, but this one was so clear!

"You will learn," it said, sounding almost like a warning. After hearing it, the whole room indulged in a collective, "Whooooa!" We all looked around at each other, trying to remember hearing anything that could have caused that arrangement of syllables. But none of us could.

So what did it mean? What would we learn? Was it something associated with the Seven Sisters Inn or someone in the room? Again, it took me some time to figure it all out, but the first piece of the puzzle came right after that session.

***

For several years prior to my stay at The Seven Sisters Inn, I experimented with EVP. Specifically, the source. Based on some reading I had done and theories I'd heard, I hypothesized that not all electronic voice phenomena were coming from spirit. Perhaps they were coming from us! By some manner of telepathy, maybe we were the cause of the phenomena we'd been assuming was coming from the Other Side.

Consider for a moment some of the common questions asked during an EVP session: What year is it? How old are you? How many are with us right now? Each of these questions prompts a numerical answer. Consequently, when playing back the recording, the listener will be expecting to hear a number in response. Even if the sound made seems like something else, most investigators will try to force that sound into one that makes sense or aligns with preconceived expectations. It's human nature to want to make order out of chaos, and it just might be fueling the phenomena. By asking a question that requires a certain type of answer, we may actually be projecting our expectations onto our recorders. But how?

When two people are face-to-face having a conversation, several processes are at work. The speaker pushes breath up the esophagus, past their teeth and tongue, which causes a vibration in the air. The listener detects that vibration with their ears, and the signal is sent to the brain, which translates it into a language we understand. We take it for granted, but many steps are involved in something as simple as a chat.

Spirit has no physical form that we're aware of, so how do they make the vibration that eludes our hearing but then appears on recording media? The current theory is that it's a psychic imprint.

Okay, so if that is the mechanism that facilitates EVPs, then why can't we produce the same result with our own minds?

I had attempted to prove that supposition but had yet to get a positive result. Still, the theory was intriguing to many at events, and it made them think about the bigger picture, which was another of my goals. With so many eager and willing participants on hand, paranormal events were the perfect place to conduct my experiment, and I did so whenever I could. That night at the Seven Sisters Inn seemed like another good opportunity to try for a positive.

***

After explaining my hypothesis, I gave the group in my Cairo Room the instructions for the experiment.

"Okay, guys, we're going to do another recording, but this time we're going to focus on one word. We'll record for sixty seconds. During that time frame, I don't want anyone to tag anything. Just focus on the word. Envision the word in your mind, picture the letters of that word emerging from your forehead and shooting towards the recorder. Do whatever you have to do to project that word mentally."

All we needed was a word, which I left to the attendees to select. After a minute or two of mumbling between the participants, a burly man with a spiked, green mohawk piped up, "How about bird? Bird is the word!" I remember his attire and hairstyle because they were quirky. In the moment, I had wondered if he was poking fun at the experiment, but he was being genuine. And what followed would cement the particulars of this attempt in my mind forever.

The group all chuckled at the word choice. It put us all in a good mood. I nodded and grinned. "Okay, so it is. Bird is the word!" I announced. "Are you ready?"

Everyone nodded, and the experiment began. After sixty seconds, it was time to listen back. I plugged in my speaker and expected the same result as every other time I had tried this experiment . . . a good effort that hopefully caused the group to consider possibilities.

"Okay, here we go," echoed my voice from the recorder, "Seven Sisters Inn, Cairo Room, the word is bird. Sixty seconds starts now."

We sat and listened to the near-silent room tone once more. Ten seconds had elapsed, and then we heard it—

"Bird," came the low whisper. Then it was followed by an even lower chant of "bird, bird, bird, bird . . ." It was a staccato-like repetition, but we all marveled at it. I had been kneeling, and the response caused me to straighten up. "Oh my God," I remember hearing one woman say, but no one was more surprised than me. I'd been conducting that experiment unsuccessfully for years and had begun to lose faith in its veracity. It had become little more than a parlor diversion to eat up time during a public hunt. But now everything had changed. This was to be the beginning of a new chapter.

We ended the session in an elevated state as the group, and I were eager to share what just happened with those in the rest of the house. As I would henceforth call it, the Psychic Projection Experiment had finally succeeded.

***

The Class A EVP from earlier that night was prophetic. I did learn something. In the weeks and months that followed, I tried to figure out why the experiment had worked this time and failed previously. The word selection seemed to have something to do with it. When picked, everyone laughed. Its humor seemed to have raised our vibrations and put us in the right state of mind. Everyone had a visceral reaction to it, and that was key. To date, I have gotten the experiment to work 40 times, and in each of those instances, the chosen word fit the new parameter. Scared, Gollum, banana, balls, and bacon are some examples, and all of them had some particular meaning or connection to those involved in the experiment.

Additionally, that night at The Seven Sisters Inn, three out of the seven people involved identified themselves as psychic. Now, while we all have psychic ability, it seems relevant that almost half of the participants were comfortable enough with that ability to raise their hands when asked. Say, if every person had a psy value of one and active psychics had a value of three, then perhaps a certain number (X) would need to be exceeded for the threshold to be crested and the imprint to take. It could be written as $\Sigma \text{ psy} > X$.

Some of you holding this book may have been present during an attempt at the Psychic Projection experiment. Some may have even witnessed a successful one. Now, allow me to put it all in the proper perspective. I've been trying this for over fifteen years, and I've only gotten it to work 40 times. That's a very low batting average. But the fact that it's worked at all is evidence that there is some merit to it. I still have a lot of work to do, but if reading this opens up your mind to possibilities, then my work thus far has not been in vain. You, too, will learn.

9
The Pendulum & the Painting

Was somebody murdered?" he asked. The room fell silent. Not a word was whispered; no one dared move an inch. All attention was focused on the bar and the man wearing the cowboy hat.

I surveyed the room as the man waited for a response. He held in his hand a chain with a cross attached at the bottom: a pendulum. It swung back and forth lazily, in no discernible or steady direction. Nearly two dozen people were gathered in this old saloon, watching the chain as it slowed to a pause.

"Are you afraid of something?" the man asked. He turned to glance at a couple standing next to him. A bespectacled man with a baseball cap had his arm around a delicate-looking woman who had her eyes closed. She appeared to be concentrating on something.

Around the room, a few K-II meters flashed, and there was the odd gasp or two, but otherwise, not much. I glanced down at my trusty Mel Meter (a custom electromagnetic field meter)—which displayed a 0.0, nothing to report as of yet. But I did feel the energy in the room start to rise.

***

It had been an interesting and enjoyable weekend so far in Tombstone, AZ. As an invited guest at the small event, I'd connected with old friends as well as made some new ones. I'd gotten to explore the old western town the day before, including the old Boot Hill Cemetery, the Birdcage Saloon, and Big Nose Kate's. I walked up and down the dusty main street, pausing from time to time to notice my altered shadow on the ground—I'd picked up a cowboy hat at one of the souvenir shops and was seldom seen without it on that trip. While everyone else was quoting the Kurt Russell movie as they traversed the town, I affixed a tin sheriff's badge to the hat and did my best Rick Grimes impression, complete with a gun draw. Oh, did I mention that my hosts had lent me a real gun to wear at my hip while I was there? Pacifist as I sometimes may be, it did feel kinda cool to have that sidearm at the ready. But fear not for the denizens of Tombstone—it was unloaded.

The investigative portion of the event was held at the Saloon Theater in Tombstone's Hoptown. After the greetings and introductory speeches, the group had gathered around the bar in the far corner of the room. Dwight and Rhonda Hull had been excellent hosts, making sure I was comfortable and deferring to me in many areas during the weekend. This time was no different. "Take it away," they said as the investigation began, then stood back to watch how I worked.

As usual, I began the formalities that evening with a group EVP session, creating the mindset that we were all on one team. Perhaps our combined efforts and intent would make it easier to connect with whatever spirits might be there. Plus, if a voice was captured on the recorder, everyone would feel like part of the experience. I can't count how many disappointed sighs I've heard at other events from investigators comparing their experiences. In their game of one-upmanship, someone always came near to being possessed—*Oh, you missed it, it was incredible!* Of course, it was. This night's EVP session in Tombstone provided a few confusing responses and one very intriguing one. Everyone had gotten a chance to ask a question, and when that was done, we listened to the recording. The one response that had us chomping at the bit to know more was: "Yeah, I killed someone." I asked the woman who'd posed the question to come to the front of the bar, closer to the recorder and the four main investigators—me, the Hulls, and the man with the cowboy hat.

Over the course of the weekend, I'd gotten to know the other three investigators a lot better. The guy in the hat was Dan Baldwin, and he was a dowser. The Hulls were historians as well as investigators. Married several decades, they also worked well together in the field; she a psychic medium, and he a researcher and a psychic/animal communicator. Several years earlier, they'd met and started working with Dan, incorporating his methodology into their own. Dan had started as an author, but one day, while researching some facts for one of his books, he came across the concept of dowsing with rods and pendulums. His fascination with the topic led him to experiment with it, and before long, he found himself quite adept at dowsing, even helping the local police with a few cases. The trio would go on to write books about their experiences and hold events like the one in which I currently found myself.

I thought it a good idea to pass the ball back to the trio, to see what more we could find out from this supposed spirit—and exactly who did what! I also wanted to see Dan use his pendulum—it was one thing to hear about it, now I wanted to see him work. Ironically, he had not brought his pendulum with him. That issue was allayed by an attendee offering up the cross she wore around her neck. One chain, one weight—we had ourselves a pendulum. The trio was now ready to go, Dan with the makeshift pendulum, Rhonda with her senses, and Dwight backing her up.

Dan's first few questions didn't seem to land anywhere, but suddenly the pendulum started to swing. I'd seen people work with them before, and I always felt like the swinging was a conscious motion. I'd see hands moving, eyes watching, things that made it so easy to remain skeptical. But not with Dan. Knowing his origins made it a bit easier for me to stay open to the possibilities. Then, seeing him in action, I only felt more at ease with the integrity of his dowsing. My eyes were fixed on his hand, which barely moved at all, and yet the pendulum had begun to move with steady intent, swinging in a wide circular motion, reaching a decent speed very rapidly. The minor fluctuations caused by breathing were all I could detect, and those were not enough to cause the pendulum to move so.

Rhonda chimed in and confirmed that we were speaking to the spirit who'd provided us with the EVP earlier. But there were others with us as well. Male energies, she reported. As well as something else . . .

"I'll ask again," Dan began. "Was somebody murdered here?"

The pendulum's circular motion came to an abrupt halt, then changed to a linear, back-and-forth one. It was as if the chain had a life of its own. According to it, someone had lost their life in this room. The audience couldn't help but react. A few "Oh, my God's" and several nods of confirmation from other sensitives in the group had us pressing on to see if we could find out who the male energies were—victims or culprits? We knew what had happened; perhaps we could figure out why and to whom. Too often in the paranormal, we come away with mere sentence fragments, and those alone keep us going, but it's rare when we have a complete tale to tell. This night we had a strong chance of doing exactly that.

"Something is over here!" cried a woman standing by the stairs.

From my vantage point behind the bar, I could see over those gathered in front of me to the staircase twenty feet away. It led up behind a trellis to a closed doorway above. No one was on, or would be coming down those steps. No one living, that is. I asked some of the other sensitives in the room to stay watchful and let me know the minute they felt a change. Currently, they were detecting three spirits with us in the room. The presence by the stairs may have been one of the men. Or perhaps it was the other energy Rhonda felt earlier.

"Is something keeping you here?" Rhonda piped up. Her eyes were still closed, and she was looking nervous.

Dan's pendulum began to swing in another direction, paused, then returned to its original pattern, almost as if something was fighting for control of it. I stepped back and took it all in. To be honest, I felt a little ineffective. With my meters reporting none of what was happening, I became a spectator in this unfolding drama. But this was not a moment to worry about ego. I was just thrilled to be present and thankful I'd chosen to keep the group together in this location (a key point from my imaginary book: *Don't Split Up the Party — And Other Things D&D Taught Me*).

As the energy in the room rose, the pace picked up. It was a palpable moment, but what would its outcome be?

"Are you the one who was killed?"

"What is your name?"

"Are you afraid of judgment?"

"Why are you holding the other one here?"

"Why did you commit that murder?"

The questions were asked furiously, and the pendulum, along with Rhonda, were doling out answers in tandem—the pendulum, binary; Rhonda, expanding on them. I'd even thrown a few of my own questions in there. I was worried that the spirits wouldn't be able to tarry too much longer. The hourglass was getting bottom-heavy for them.

The information we'd gotten so far was that the two men were involved in a murder here at the bar. Of the two spirits, one was dominant; the other was subservient to him. They came as a pair. The third energy was feminine and seemed to be that of a helper spirit, who was here to assist in bringing them to the next phase. She let us know the other two had been here for quite a while, stuck.

Whether intentionally or by accident, the dominant male had done the deed. He'd killed someone and was afraid to move on because of it. Unwilling to be alone, he kept the lesser spirit there with him. The strain of guilt and seemingly endless years stuck in this bar had taken a toll on both of their psyches, which seemed to back up what researchers have theorized over the years about earthbound spirits: if they chose to stay for whatever reason, it did not come without a price. And for investigators, much like speaking to a mentally ill patient in an asylum, a conversation with earthbound spirits didn't always go smoothly.

"How can we help you?" I asked.

We had gotten as many facts as the spirits seemed willing to share. As far as interrogations went, this one had gone better than I could have hoped for, but as with any story, it needed an ending. Not only did I sense the spirits losing energy, but I also saw the gathered investigators, and especially our main trio, running low. Dwight pulled Rhonda close to him as if to give her all his remaining strength to carry on. Dan nodded to the two of them. They were running through their playbook. It was time to bring their endgame.

"You don't have to stay here. Don't be afraid. It is safe," Rhonda instructed.

All around us, the air got thin. It was as if everyone stopped breathing for a moment for fear of disrupting the connection we had made.

"It's okay," Dan started, "you can let—" He was cut off. The pendulum, which had been energetically swinging back and forth, jerked suddenly and then came to a near stop. It was as if someone had yanked its power cord out from the wall. "He's gone," he said.

Rhonda nodded in agreement. They had all gone.

I was dumbfounded. Everyone else let out a sigh of relief, finally able to breathe again. We all looked at each other for a moment. I turned to one of the attendees, a friend of mine; her eyes were glassy. Her friend next to her was searching for a tissue. Everyone seemed to be similarly affected. I turned back to Dan and the Hulls.

"Did what I think just happened, happen?" I inquired.

Without a pause, Rhonda confidently responded, "Yes, they all went into the light."

That was a big statement to make. Could it be true? Was I just present for the crossing over of multiple spirits into the Afterlife?

For the next few minutes, we all replayed and discussed what had transpired. A few people went outside for air, others for a smoke, but the majority, like me, felt compelled to dwell in the moment for a bit longer. I know many out there claim to be in the business of "Spirit Rescue" and run around crossing over as many as possible. But that's not me. I'm a researcher. As I said before, I want information. I'm an observer, and as such, I try not to influence the outcome of the situation. If others do it all the time, that's great, but for me, this was a unique experience, one I don't take lightly.

How can I describe an experience I could only feel on an extra-sensory level? As the questions were being asked and answered, it was like a balloon being inflated. The more information we got, the more air was inside the balloon, making it harder to inflate and increasing the chance it might pop. Speaking of which, when the pendulum suddenly stopped, I could have sworn I heard a muffled popping sound. Whether from the connection being lost or the spirits passing over, there was an audible sound to accompany it. And I wasn't the only one to hear it.

***

I had always been skeptical of pendulums and quite honestly thought of dowsing as a sloppy avenue of investigation, conducted mostly by amateurs wanting to jumpstart their reputations, or by psychics receiving information through other means and using dowsing tools for confirmation. Either way, I didn't think it was for me—until that night. The Crossing Over at Tombstone had me seriously reconsidering. Dan gave me some pointers on how to use a pendulum. He also dispelled many of the misconceptions I had about the practice. All I had to do now was get myself one.

The task turned out to be easy enough as I was often gifted items at events from various vendors. When I got home from Tombstone, I dug around on my metaphysical shelf (where I put all my minerals, gemstones, and "those items" that I've gathered over the years). There, in a small wooden box, I found a hematite pendulum. Ironically, I'd once been asked which type of stone spoke to me the most, and I'd answered hematite. Now, about that universal plan . . .

Excited to try it out after what I had learned, I brought the pendulum over to the window. I took a deep breath and held it out before me.

"Show me yes," I said. After a moment or two, it started to move in a pattern, lightly at first and then stronger. I thanked it and grabbed the stone to stop it and bring it back to center.

"Show me no." The same thing happened, albeit in a different pattern. My basic responses had been set.

I was amazed by the swiftness of these responses. My skeptical nature surprisingly allowed me a moment of elation over the fact that I had gotten it to work. I couldn't say how, but after repeating the opening exercise a number of times, the responses stayed steady each time.

Of course, I had to put it to the test. I'm always in a battle with myself, so my snarky, skeptical side had to step in for the inaugural question. I couldn't ask anything I knew, like my favorite color or something I could see around me. I also didn't want to connect with any spirits or call any to my home. I've always refused to practice at home—I like my quiet too much to have my apartment become a spectral Grand Central Station.

So, I decided to do a little forecasting. Perhaps I was inspired by that tarot card reader from years back (see Chapter Four - It's in the Cards). She'd been right when she read her cards—*Haunted Collector* was proof of that—maybe I'd be able to see what was coming with my pendulum.

Taking another deep breath, I centered myself.

"Will I ever get back on television," I asked. Aware that I left a lot of latitude for answers I did not mean, I asked again and clarified. "Will I ever be cast again on a paranormal television show?" Almost immediately, the pendulum began to swing. It wasn't a lackluster swing either; it was a strong response in the affirmative.

My eyebrows raised at the news. *Oh, really?* I thought. That was nice to hear, but of course, my second thought was that my desire to be back on television had unconsciously influenced my hand to somehow deliver the result. I don't know why I would want to lie to myself, but the thought was there all the same. The joy of getting the item to work perhaps created the need not to have that joy dispelled so soon after. Perhaps a follow-up question would decide.

"Will I make a lot of money doing it?" I asked apprehensively.

Like buying a lottery ticket, when you hope to win but don't really expect to, that was the feeling that accompanied this question—a cautious optimism. And, like checking your lottery ticket days later and finding that none of your numbers match, the pendulum's swing to the negative brought a morbid disappointment. I mean, it wasn't like I'd just found out I had cancer. I was asking a rock tied to a string about my future in entertainment! But it was disappointing all the same. Perhaps I should have asked a Magic 8 Ball and hoped for an "Ask Again Later." Satisfied that I could use and consult my pendulum in the future, I put it away. Since that day, I've never used it to ask questions about myself, only ones about a case or investigating a haunted location.

I've surprised myself at how adept I've gotten at the practice. It usually comes with the caveat that I don't know how it works or why it works, but only that it does, and since I have no stake in the outcome, it must be authentic. Testing my skills on tour in Northern Ireland, my hosts from Team Blue of Ghost Searchers Ireland assisted me. I instructed someone to stand behind me and hold up a certain number of fingers on one hand. They did so, and after going through the numbers as the pendulum responded, I arrived at the correct one. Once, twice, three times. I kept delivering the right answer. One of their more skeptical team members circled me and examined the surroundings to see if I might be coming by the information another way. Then he decided to insert himself into the next trial, and it had an unexpected effect.

"Okay, hold up a few fingers on one hand," I instructed again.

I cleared the pendulum and began at one. A negative response. "Two fingers?" I asked it. The pendulum shook oddly as if it was confused, then came back as yes. The voice behind me said I was wrong.

"Keep them up; I'll keep going," I said. It sucks to be wrong when you're being put to the test, but I knew better than to consider myself infallible with this new tool. "Three fingers?" Negative. "Four?" Once again, the pendulum wavered as it seemed to be considering its report. Then it swung in the affirmative.

"Nope," came the voice again.

"Oh, come on now," interjected a teammate, "you're trying to trick him, and that's not fair."

I turned around to see what they were talking about, expecting to see a big foam hand or some other funny item. Instead, the resident Team Blue skeptic stood behind me with both of his hands up, each of them with two fingers extended. I had no idea he'd done this or even considered that it was a possibility as I asked my numerical queries of the pendulum, and yet it seemed to have been right! I was focusing on the number of fingers being held up behind me, but I had assumed it was on one hand. Since he'd used both hands, each with two fingers up, the pendulum had been technically correct by delivering positive results for both two and four. I was just being unclear about the parameters of the question. This moment taught me to be super clear with my pendulum questions, even repeating and rephrasing them when multiple interpretations are possible.

As I mentioned, I had no ego to bruise when it came to wrong answers, but at the same time, I wanted to perform at my best when utilizing the pendulum. I had to learn to separate myself from the situation and just be a conduit for the information. Was that what psychics did when they communicated with spirit? Continued work with my pendulum has seen me evolve in a way I never thought I would within The Work. As a paranormal postal worker of sorts!

I've found myself at events lately, taking out my pendulum as a change of pace from the over-saturation of gadgets. Plus, no ghost could ever drain the batteries on a device that required none to operate. The public does delight in the surprise of seeing the tech guy they know from TV pull out a metaphysical tool to investigate. And I must admit that I never thought I'd be doing this either. If the Brian from 2002 could see the Brian of today, using a pendulum of all things, I have no doubt he'd hit me with a few harsh words. But as I expressed in the last chapter, that's the beautiful thing about harboring ideas and not clinging to beliefs—we can all change and grow in the face of new information.

In the past, I would introduce the concept of dowsing via a pendulum, tell an anecdote or two to eat up time, then make a few attempts to connect and get information. But lately, I've been using my pendulum in a different capacity. One night, instead of asking about the location we were investigating, I asked if a spirit had a message for anyone gathered there. The response came through in the positive. Surprised, I went about "bringing in the box," a technique Dan had taught me that involved starting general and then narrowing questions until specific details could be obtained. A message came through for an attendee from a deceased family member. I was careful to be sensitive to the personal nature of some of the questions. At one point, I recalled my experience in Tombstone and thought it best to turn the questions over to that person, so they could ask whatever they needed. It was an intimate experience, a shared moment between us all, and it served as validation for something greater than ourselves—the knowledge that love survives death. The tears shed by the message recipient represented the champagne bottle breaking over the bow of my new function as a deliverer of messages from beyond. Who knew? From that day forward, a personal message for someone has come through at almost every function where I've taken the pendulum out. It's as if departed spirits somehow have my number and can queue to talk when my pendulum comes out.

My new role as messenger was never more strongly confirmed than at a recent paranormal convention. As I met and chatted with con-goers stopping by my table, I noticed many of them had small paintings with an interesting composition. Splashes of color were juxtaposed with rivers of black to form images that seemed to move as you looked at them. It turned out that each one was a custom piece done by a psychic artist in one of the other vendor rooms. He would do an energy reading of each person and then paint what he saw—an artistic representation of the information he was presented with. I found the method fascinating—not only did the person come away with a reading, but a souvenir that could be displayed and shared with others on several levels. It appealed to my creative nature, so I decided I would take the time to get one of my own before the weekend was over. I joked with friends as they stopped by—many of whom had already received their energy interpretations—that mine would probably be black and garish. I wasn't far off.

Approaching the psychic artist's table, I saw a middle-aged man with shoulder-length blonde hair in a black sport coat holding a paintbrush. He resembled actor Donal Logue, which strangely put me at ease. His eyes were closed as he hovered over a tiny canvas, perhaps deep in thought. A pair of white earbuds trailed down from his ears to an iPod sitting on the table. His head twitched, not to a beat, but as if he were an android calculating odds. A woman sat silently in a chair before him, apparently the subject of the current reading. Suddenly, his eyes flared open, and he began to paint. With staccato strokes and an intense focus, he had the appearance of an orchestra conductor as he worked on his alla prima symphony. Moments later, he was done. Breathing out a sigh, he sat back and looked at his creation. He spoke a few words to the woman, set the painting aside to dry, and told her to pick it up later. She thanked him with a hug and then left.

It was then my turn to sit with Brian Danhausen. He greeted me warmly and explained his process. Taking my hands in his, he told me he would spend the next few moments reading my energy. The snapshot he would get would be anchored in the now. It would have roots in the past and offer some glimpse into the immediate future, but he could only pass on what was shown to him. I nodded my understanding and prepared to be read. Often, in the past, I'd get tense and try to throw up mental walls to resist being read, but this time was different. I just let the energy flow. I wanted his reading and my painting to be as accurate as possible.

As I'd seen him do with the woman, he closed his eyes and seemed to be downloading information. For a brief moment, I imagined a progress bar above his head, slowly filling up. It made me smile. I wondered if that moment of mirth would be detected and alter the reading. Perhaps, I thought, I should recall favorite comedians and run through their routines in my head. Or maybe think of kittens—not a good call. I thought of my departed cat Beadie, and immediately the mirth was gone. The acute sadness of loss had canceled out the laughter in my mind.

Brian's twitching continued. I realized my erratic thoughts were probably confusing him—making my energy spike and wane rapidly. My intention to sit still and let the energy flow wasn't working, but perhaps that was for the best. I'd always had a hard time shutting my brain off. That was who I was, so he'd be getting a pure read, ups and downs and all.

After a few minutes, his eyes opened. His expression was one of urgency. Like John Coffey in *The Green Mile*, he had taken in something and needed to regurgitate it, in this case, onto the canvas. He put his earbuds in and began to paint. I could not see the painting as it was being done, only the motion of his hands.

I dwelled in this moment of creation, adjacent to its architect. All around me were people talking, selling things, and making connections. The convention was in full swing, but I had it on mute. It was as if Brian hadn't yet released me from our connection. Looking to my left, I admired the pictures set out to dry for other attendees. Blues, oranges, and the occasional green danced across the images. Abstract interpretations of "self" dominated the centers of most of the works. Colorful details along the edges told a story unique to the person it was meant for. I was eager to see mine. Soon, it was ready.

Brian prepared me once again by saying that this was what he saw in the present moment and, as such, was open to interpretation. He would walk me through it and answer any questions I had.

He turned the easel around to reveal a vision of darkness. A black background was broken up by a hellish red glow at the center, in front of which stood a figure painted black. His eyes were blue, and at the center of his chest was a red circle. He stood on a pathway leading forward in one direction. On the bottom and around the sides were shadowy forms, all reaching out. Hovering above to the left was a wispy white form with arms or wings that appeared to be trying to surround him.

I had joked about how my painting would look, and this night-marish scene of blacks, reds, and white had me speechless for a moment. I very much wanted to hear his take. I was familiar with the demons running around in my head, but I'd never had that angst printed out before. Brian could read my reaction and began to explain.

"It's not as bad as it seems," he started. "The figure in the middle is you. Given the work you do, you walk down some dark roads. It is the path you have chosen. The eyes are blue; that is how I see male energy."

"What is that red shape on my chest?" I asked.

"That means you're alive," he responded.

"Whew, well, that is good news, isn't it! What about all these figures around me? They're pretty scary looking."

Brian hesitated a moment as he considered his words. "Those are the dead." From the look on his face, I felt certain that mine had turned a few shades whiter. He put his hands out to indicate he wasn't finished. "They are there because of your chosen path. You are in a spot where they are coming to you for help."

That made me feel a little better. The black forms had white eyes and appeared to be grasping at me.

"But you have to be careful," he added. "Not all of them are good. See here; this one has claws—doing what you do, you leave yourself open and are at risk of attack by the darker elements."

I saw the one he pointed out. Like a wolf in sheep's clothing, coming to me for help but bearing a dagger, it was hidden in plain sight amongst the others. I inspected the shapes closer. As a whole, they appeared dangerous, like an uncontrollable mob. Looking at each one individually, however, I could see the attitudes and postures of each. Some wanted help. The figure at the center could cure their loneliness and suffering. Was that truly me? Others simply wanted to be acknowledged. My eyes drew once again to the white figure, and I noticed that it had red eyes.

"This is a protector," Brian continued. "I paint female energy with red eyes. This figure is here to watch over you. It's unclear if it is a spirit guide, one of the dead, or a person in your life, but they are there for you if you call upon them."

Initially, the red eyes worried me, as traditionally, the bad guys have red eyes. But looking at it again, I saw things differently. The outstretched arms weren't trying to envelop me; they were keeping the shadows at bay. Sometimes possessiveness causes us to smother the very things we try to protect. This was the opposite. This was a selfless act of protection.

Perspective is an amazing thing. It truly does color the reality around us. When I first saw the painting, my heart sank as if I were about to receive dire news. After hearing Brian's interpretation of it, I instead felt hopeful, even proud of the reading. Knowing that others saw me as one who could help was reassuring.

I thought about my recent work with the pendulum and the personal messages I was helping pass along. Perhaps it was true, not only the pendulum but all of my efforts in the paranormal field. Maybe I was making a difference. As hard as the paranormal road can be, with its twists and turns, with the obstacles and backstabbers, with the dues you have to pay over and over again, just the knowledge that it matters makes it all worthwhile. So I trudge on.

I still haven't used my pendulum to ask about my future again. Incidentally, though, I am back on television. And no, I'm not making a lot of money. Fate is not without its sense of humor.

10

The Battle of Poasttown

We all crawl around in the dark, looking for answers, search-ing for truth. That search often takes us to interesting places and introduces us to interesting people. Many get hung up with collecting "evidence" to prove a supposition, but in reality, all they do is gather experiences. In some way, the personal experience is evidence, but it is also subject to change. Change in the telling and change in the way it is received.

Due to the subjective nature of interpretation, it is difficult to lock down what we term as evidence. There is no picture I could show, no video clip, no sound file that would be enough to convince some-one who refuses to believe. Even if one was inclined to believe, the burden of proof still rests on the presenter, and no matter how con-vincing the evidence is, it can be undone by one simple statement: I wasn't there.

Without observing the phenomena directly, one has to consider the presenter and decide if they are worthy of belief. Ironically, it comes down to faith. I show you that picture or video, and you have to choose to either believe me or not. My reputation and the expla-nation, as well as the veracity of said evidence, all factor into that choice. The point then becomes clear—that the personal experience must be considered evidence as well, because it too was not experi-enced by the person hearing the tale, and yet it happened. It took me a while to understand this. It took what I jokingly refer to as "a mild possession" to really wake me up to it all.

***

It was the summer of 2014, and I found myself in a very hot gymnasium in Ohio. Specifically, the gymnasium of Poasttown Elementary School, where the paranormal event was taking place. It was not unlike other events I'd attended. Assorted vendor booths were hawking all manner of wares, from votive candles to electronic gear and more. Several para-celebs, including me, stood behind tables with our 8x10 photos laid out, ready to greet the attendees. The room was a sea of banners displaying names, logos, and stern faces with folded arms (the typical investigator pose). But one thing made this event different. It was a feeling that had been sparked by a Facebook post a week and a half earlier.

In the days leading up to any event, the presence on social media intensifies as excitement builds. Likes and posts of "Can't wait!!" or "See you there!" fill up the timelines of countless pages. This time was no different, except for the addition of the following: "Bring your Nerf guns."

Bring your Nerf guns? What exactly did that mean? Beyond the merch and excitement, our event staples typically included moonshine and drama. Now we were arming up?

The comment had received many likes as well as many boasts. No one questioned it, though. Neither did I. I just made sure to pack my Zombie Strike Crossbow and Hammer Shotgun. Thinking about it now, I find it funny that I even had a Nerf gun to bring, much less several.

So there we all were in the school gymnasium, patiently waiting for the public to arrive. To be gentle, the event was scarcely attended, so much of the day was spent catching up with our booth neighbors. It was a friendly atmosphere, but there was an unusual tension in the air. Perhaps it was frustration with the low attendance. Maybe it was the heat. Maybe it was something else.

As I recall, the room got quiet for a moment, like the instant before a summer storm hits. There was a certain electricity in the air, and then it happened. *WHIZ!* A Nerf dart zipped horizontally across my field of vision! That's all it took. One dart.

Just like in the third act of the movie *Hot Fuzz*, the whole room erupted into gunfire. Nerf gunfire, that is. Everyone drew their weapons and began shooting indiscriminately in every direction. To view the sudden chaos from afar may have made it seem as if a flash mob had taken over the room. There was no period of escalation or hesitation; the dial simply started at eleven. Darts whizzed by from all directions, some hitting me, others impacting on my banner behind me. I took cover behind my table and scrambled about to recover spent rounds on the floor. Fifty feet to my right, I could see one of the black shirt paranormal group members advancing towards me, zig-zagging between tables. The weapons I had brought required two different ammo types—one took darts, the other discs. I kept the latter on my belt as a "just in case" measure since I wouldn't be able to reload once the discs were spent (no one else seemed to be using those). Forty feet. Thirty feet. His advancement seemed to be meeting no opposition.

I crouched to the floor and tried to hide. Looking to my left, I saw an option. There was a path through the metal folding chairs and stacked cardboard boxes of merch that would allow me to evade my oncoming attacker. My booth was situated up against a side wall of the gym. The stage was over to the left, with the exit door to the left of that. Twenty feet, he was almost upon me. I could hear the cries of battle echoing throughout the high-ceilinged room. The time to move was now!

On my hands and knees, I crawled over to the corner of the next booth. I only had one dart remaining on my crossbow. I jumped up and fired at the black shirt, momentarily halting his advancement, then ducked back down. I scurried along the floor behind my neighbor's table—they were nowhere to be found, so I encountered no resistance—and as I got to the front corner of the room, I saw another empty booth diagonally across from mine where I could take cover. The enemy had not yet taken my table, as he had gotten attacked from the side. I saw my window of opportunity.

It's funny now to recall having such tunnel vision for this one assailant and him for me. A battle raged on around us, with many targets, but we seemed so intent on our eventual clash that nothing else mattered. Making it to the empty booth diagonal from mine, I drew my Hammer Shot. It was loaded with five discs. I had my adversary flanked and was in a good position for an ambush. The scene continued in slow motion as I stood up and fired, holding the gun like Rick Grimes from the Walking Dead and unloading all five discs with no hesitation. Two of the five hit their mark while the others sailed off into the room. He had no chance to respond as he slid and hit the floor.

"WHOA!! CEASE FIRE!!" came the shout from Darrell, the event organizer. "We have people coming! Everyone get ready!"

Darrell was a big burly man who spoke softly and always wore an Aloha shirt with too many buttons undone. I'd never heard him raise his voice before, but the sound of it stopped us all dead in our tracks. Like a splash of cold water, it brought us to our senses. All combatants picked up their ammo, straightened out their tables, and resumed a state of professional readiness.

It was a very strange moment. I could feel my face a little flushed, and I felt confused, even a little embarrassed by how caught up I'd become in such frivolous activity when I was supposed to represent myself and the field. I don't know what came over me. At least I wasn't alone in it.

The day carried on much like the first half. A lot of standing around, a lot of staring. At one point, the black shirt paranormal group marched by on their way to the exit. My one-time opponent nodded and winked as he passed. I grinned. It was kind of funny how it all went down, a shared moment to talk about later. I also sensed, however, that this powder keg was destined to explode again; it was just a question of when.

A short time later, the black shirts returned, and the arms race had escalated! They strolled in carrying what appeared to be a Nerf cannon wrapped in a Wal Mart bag that could barely contain the edges of the box. This thing was impressive. I could see that they'd bought several packages of ammo as well. The wink my opponent had given me on the way out was replaced by a shit-eating grin that clued me into where that cannon would be aimed. Their table was on the other side of the gym, opposite from the stage, but it looked like I was still within striking distance of their new armament.

I sat down and started sorting through the rounds I had recovered from the last sortie. I figured, if nothing else, he who had the most ammo would be in a better bargaining position should hostility erupt again. But now, my tiny ammo seemed irrelevant as I faced my own personal Cuban Missile Crisis. So I waited. And waited. And nothing happened. Hours went by, and it seemed like the morning's incident would not repeat itself. I'd forgotten about it, truth be told, until I saw something orange hit the wall to my right.

Time slowed once again as I turned my head to see where it came from. On the far end of the gym, I could see a portly man with a Nerf gun in both hands, firing at a girl with glasses who was laughing and running for cover. Darts arced in every direction, creating a sort of foam firework pattern in the air. I was momentarily mesmerized by the basic beauty of the scene. Alliteration aside, I thought it was pretty cool and felt a childlike excitement over round two of this battle. Then a dart hit me right in the eye!

"Goddammit! Now you're gonna pay!" I groaned.

The joyfulness had passed, and now there was only warfare. This time no one stayed at their tables. Everyone ran around the room, shooting and laughing, ducking and taunting.

"I hit you!" one girl shouted.

"No, you didn't, that totally missed!" responded another.

I paused for a moment to observe one woman at the center of the fracas, anxiety abundant in her eyes as she attempted to shield the stemware on her table. She let out a high-pitched shriek as a large red dart came close to striking a painted wine glass. I should have felt concerned for her, an innocent amidst a skirmish. She was unarmed, had many delicate items on her table, and was clearly unprepared to handle such an unexpected turn of events. Maybe she didn't see the same Facebook post I did.

None of that registered for long as the more important question forced its way to the forefront of my mind. Who had fired that huge dart?

"Hey, Cano!" came the shout from across the room. I glanced over my shoulder and winced. The black shirts had their cannon loaded and ready. I could see the auxiliary barrel of ammo attached to the side, holding a ton of large, red darts. They were easily twice the size of the regular ones. And it was pointed at me. Oh, crap.

I hit the deck as a barrage of red missiles came whizzing by my head. The sound they made as they flew through the air distinguished them from the smaller ones already being fired. The big gun had literally arrived. No one or nothing was safe from its range, and it was as if the gym had become a shooting gallery. The sound those hard plastic tips made upon impact was like boxing gloves hitting a speedbag. All you could do was duck for cover.

I found another unoccupied table and turned it on its side. A couple of other combatants joined me behind it. The mega darts pelted it like rain on a roof, and we knew we'd incur casualties if we tried to fire back. But just then, we heard a break in the barrage. A brief silence instilled hope in our breasts. They had to reload . . .

"Now's our chance, boys! CHARGE!" I cried out. We all know that the nail that sticks out furthest will always get hammered down. Also, men often put aside their differences and unite to fight a bigger, common enemy. That's human nature. All these tropes and social norms served me well as I stood and leaped over the table. The others streamed around the sides. A united front counter attacked the black shirt cannon as they fumbled to reload. It could have been my imagination, but the first movement of the Carmina Burana was playing somewhere in the background as we advanced on the back wall. It seemed as if our victory would be assured when . . .

"OKAY, THAT'S ENOUGH!" Darrell shouted. "You guys have to settle down. More people are coming." His tone of voice was strained; his patience nearly run out.

Once again, the splash of cold water hit us all, and we cleaned up and returned to normalcy. But this time, my embarrassment lingered. We were all running around recklessly, like children. So much so that we risked damaging other people's property with our tomfoolery.

"Sorry, Darrell," I muttered. "Bring 'em down. We're ready."

The event continued and transitioned into the night portion, where mini investigations of the school were taking place. I explored for a bit but then stationed myself in a classroom and conducted EVP sessions with all who joined me. Usually, during EVP sessions, participants spoke up with morbid inquiries like "When did you die?" or "Are you trapped here?" But on this night, because we were in a classroom, the questions mostly centered around teachers and students. They were generally more positive, and most attendees phrased their questions as if they were talking to children. That wasn't a surprise, given the location. Additionally, the reports associated with the place regaled tales of ghostly children running through the hallways, and child-like voices heard in some of the rooms.

As I write this, it seems glaringly obvious what had happened earlier that day, in the gymnasium, but at the time, it just did not register. Poasttown Elementary was a school that saw thousands of children pass through its doors over the years. There'd been laughter and tears, excitement and wonder. Fresh minds were beginning to grow. Social constructs were beginning to form. It was a time when it was still acceptable to play—until the teacher told you it was time to stop.

My point is this: Death wasn't required to stir up a haunting at Poasttown Elementary. The energy left behind by all the children and even the teachers was more than enough. We'd gotten possible child responses during our EVP sessions, but the residual energy was something we definitely felt. Not during the investigation—but during the day!

Rare is the moment when you can walk into an active elementary school gymnasium and find kids quiet and at attention. More often than not, you'll find a cacophony of motion as kids run around playing, expending the endless well of energy that children seem to possess. If any event attendees had walked into the gym during our Nerf war, it might have looked very much the same.

In my embarrassment over Darrell having to come in repeatedly and scold us all like children, I kept asking myself what had come over me? I didn't understand why I had acted that way. It was so unlike me. Don't get me wrong: I had fun and enjoyed every minute of it, but it was not the way I—or any of us—ever acted at an event. It had never happened before, and it has never happened since, and it took me a few weeks of reflection to realize that we all may have experienced a mild possession. I'm not talking about demonic possession. Rather, I think we all absorbed some of that juvenile energy, and it allowed us to drop our guards for a bit. It allowed us to be silly and play and just be in the moment, just like children. I had felt the excitement of competition, the thrill of motion, and the joy of laughing during it all. I hadn't felt that in a long time. It taught me a bit about spirit and ourselves as human beings, and it reinforced my premise that not every haunting need be negative.

The Battle of Poasttown lasted for only one afternoon in the summer of 2014. It ended with zero casualties. But it left a lasting impression on all who participated.

11

Strange Times at Spirit Springs

'd never really believed in curses. The supernatural kind, that is. An arrangement of beliefs designed to deliver a specific outcome for an intended target, the word alone conjures up images of kerchiefed old women with warts on their noses and black cats (who have gotten an unfair rap, I might add—the cats, not the women) at their side. Be it from the Evil Eye, a Voodoo priestess, or another source, the thought of having a malediction placed on you has affected people's behavior for generations.

We've all heard of the Mummy's Curse, also known as the Curse of the Pharaohs, which allegedly causes bad luck, illness, or death to anyone who disturbs the mummified remains of an Egyptian person—especially a pharaoh. Less exotic but seemingly just as feared are Germanic hexes that have traditionally targeted farm animals' health and, in turn, a farmer's livelihood. Personally, I'd never found myself digging around in Egypt, nor in the business of animal husbandry, so the concept of a curse always seemed far away. It was something that happened to other people, if it happened at all. Today, I'm not so sure.

Over the years, Chris and I have joked with one another about a *SCARED!* curse, something that kept us from collecting the rewards of our efforts. If any windfall were to come our way, it was immediately followed by a reversal of fortune that twisted the knife. It always felt specific and targeted, like someone out there had it in for us. It was akin to finding a ten-dollar bill in a washed pair of jeans, only to walk outside and find a $55 parking ticket on your car.

We wore this "curse" like a badge of honor, a scar of experience. We'd even laugh about it when things went south and mutter, "Yep. *SCARED!* Curse." It even became a card in the Extreme Hauntings expansion of The Three Pillars card game. Terridus (Latin for scared) is one of the most paralyzing cards in the set. One thing is certain: We can't be accused of not making fun of our failings.

I've recently popped up on TV a few times in conjunction with a place called Oak Island, which allegedly is under a curse regarding a treasure buried somewhere on it. I was tapped to offer my opinion, but I am by no means an expert. In my research and exploration, I've come across a lot of information on the topic of curses, but so much of it is rooted in the intangible that it's hard to accept. However, what seems consistent is the notion that in order for a curse to work, the recipient has to believe in it. It can also be a wider cultural phenomenon, as seen in such superstitions as the Curse of the Bambino. This particular one saw the Boston Red Sox unable to win a World Series for 86 years after trading Babe Ruth to the New York Yankees. In this situation, why would a curse have been generated, and by whom?

We have a cursory understanding about the Universe, that it's all energy and vibration. It has laws that hold it together and make it work, kind of like The Force in *Star Wars*. Well, at least I find it fun to equate it to that. But here's the thing: Of all the invisible forces in our world—x-rays, gamma rays, radiation, and more—none requires our belief in it to work. Take gravity, for example. It just works. Disbelieving in it will not allow you to break its laws. If you step out of a window, you will fall—that's just a fact.

But what about curses? Do they actually work? And what if one is placed on a non-believer? Are they safe from its effects, or will they just explain away any event that could be caused by it? So many questions.

Regarding our self-styled *SCARED!* curse, a mentor of mine would joke that he often would be affected by it when we were around. That concerned me despite its flippant delivery. While he later consoled us that we were fine, he also added that the Law of Attraction dictated that our expectations could cause some of the instances we ascribed to a curse. So for us, it was less of a jinx and more of a self-fulfilling prophecy.

Okay, we were our own worst enemies; that was not news to us. But offensive imprecations were still a topic that needed examination. What makes them so worrisome is that they are meant to cause trouble or harm to the people they're placed upon. There are no happy curses. They are the exact opposite of blessings and can adversely affect individuals, locations, as well as families. Really nasty ones can affect multiple generations. They can even come attached to innocent-looking items. And, as I was about to learn, sometimes to some not-so-innocent looking ones . . .

***

For weeks things had felt strange on the road with *Haunted Collector*. We were doing case after case in rapid succession, filming episodes for our second season. Fatigue was beginning to set in and had caused us all to be rather muted. I enjoyed the travel, but even I could feel it. Beyond the rigors of a tight schedule, we had been dealing with the paranormal side effects of all these cases, not to mention dragging around a case of collected items that John would eventually deposit into his museum. And we were about to come across an item that stands out to this day as one of the most chilling on the show.

We had been summoned to Winchester, VA, to help the owner of the Historic Jordan Springs Event & Cultural Centre, who'd been experiencing all manners of negative activity. The property was located on a naturally occurring sulfur spring regarded as sacred by Native Americans due to the water's high mineral content. Originally a spa and hotel where American elite, including Franklin Roosevelt and others, visited to bathe in the spring's supposed healing waters, the conference center had also been used as a Civil War hospital, a brothel, a monastery, and a rehab center for teens. Needless to say, much had occurred there over the years!

Tonie told us about all the things she had experienced in her eleven years owning the place. In the ballroom, she'd heard a boy's voice, doors would swing open and slam shut, and often she'd come in to find chairs moved around. In her office, formerly a chapel, she'd experienced odd schisms of perception, like witnessing an employee at her door who, she later found out, hadn't left his desk in hours. Shadow figures, phantom footsteps, and disembodied female voices were common occurrences there. Upstairs in the billiards room, a visitor had been choked, growls had been heard, and a radio would suspiciously turn on by itself. Specific personalities, such as a Civil War nurse and a monk, had been seen by several witnesses throughout the property.

Tonie said that while these things seemed strange, she had gotten used to them. But lately, things had gotten more intense. Several months before she called us, an earthquake struck the area, the first to shake this part of Virginia in centuries. On top of that, a large storm had hit weeks prior, and a tornado touched down in the woods behind the building. It cut a swath of destruction for several hundred feet before dissipating. These two events coincided with the activity getting stronger, but she couldn't figure out why.

"Could we be dealing with elementals?" I asked John as we drove to the set.

The Old Man looked incredulously at me. "How do you know about those?" he replied.

It was nice to know I could occasionally surprise him. Want to know a secret? I knew about elementals from playing Dungeons & Dragons. I had guessed about their actuality, and his reaction confirmed it for me. But I wasn't going to reveal my hand to John. Oh, the things the Monster Manual had taught me over the years!

The past few cases we'd done all seemed to have common themes—one centered around water, another around fire. This one had elements of earth and air surrounding it (the earthquake and tornado). I'm always looking for patterns. Here, I was trying to find a governing force that could link all of these cases. I'm also a completist, so having all of the basic elements under one explanation would have been quite satisfying. Neatly wrapped up with a bow on top. Alas, it was not meant to be. There were, however, other revelations in store.

Each of us had our own experiences as the investigation commenced. Some of the highlights were seen in the episode, but as usual, there were too many to put them all in. That's often frustrating for us, and I know it's frustrating for viewers, but in defense of the producers, they're trying to arrange our experiences into an entertaining storyline. They're not trying to make a documentary or prove the existence of the afterlife. Therefore, many of the experiences and pieces of evidence that don't lead to the "story's" conclusion are left out. In this case, even members of the production crew had experiences!

Several of the cameramen reported seeing shadows darting around corners and feeling as if they were being watched. One night, after a tough day on set and dealing with his higher-ups, one of the executive producers returned to the hotel to find his bathroom infested with locusts. I'll never forget the worried look on his face when he found John and me in the lobby. He stumbled over his words as he asked for an explanation and advice. I watched his exchange with John silently. It was like a sick man asking a doctor what was wrong and pleading for it not to be terminal. I mused that including these types of bits in the show would improve it greatly, but I knew those thoughts were folly.

I've noticed recently that some shows have gotten smarter in that respect. If something happens to a cameraman or sound tech, they'll acknowledge and include it. It was never so with us, unfortunately. Orders came from the network to stick to the formula, and at times it was annoyingly rigid. One example that comes to mind happened after a case we did in Joplin, MO. John had gotten suddenly and violently ill, ghost sickness perhaps. But whatever it was, it had him incapacitated and unable to film for a couple of days. I recall standing outside the hospital with that same executive producer who'd had locusts in his bathroom and listening to him panic about the schedule. To fall behind was to throw the entire season off, and that would incur costs. We all know that the almighty dollar often sidelines the quest for truth. I had an idea that would satisfy both needs.

"Let's use this," I began, "and show how the team copes with their leader being down." I went on to pitch how it would be a great next episode. With John being out of commission due to a prior case, it would be up to the rest of the team to carry on and see if our training had been sufficient. Imagine that! An episode of *Haunted Collector* where we had to go it alone, without the guidance of our esteemed mentor—it would make for great television. I told the producer it would be like *Charlie's Angels*, where John would send us out on the mission but not actually be there. Then, in the end, we'd return home with an item and have him evaluate our performance. Not only would it show the growth of other cast members, but it would also shine a light on the potential consequences of The Work. I considered it a genius idea. The executive producer nodded and agreed, but in a tone of voice I had come to know so well, he indicated there was no way in hell he was going to suggest my idea to SyFy. They propped John up to get his intro segments and OTFs (On the fly interviews) at the tail end of the next shoot. As it must, the show went on.

That's why any deviation from routine was a welcome one. Our second to last night at Jordan Springs found us in the facility's lower level, in a basement bar, seated at a round table. The whole team had gathered to conduct a group EVP session, which was a rarity on the show. The cameras rolled, and one by one, we began asking questions. The energy in the room began to coalesce. As I looked around the table, I could see in the eyes of my castmates that something was about to happen. We all felt it, but what was it? As seen in the episode, activity occurred that redirected our attention to the door leading outside. Whispers, light taps, and then knocks brought us to our feet.

To this day, I cannot tell you exactly what led us there. I can't explain why we were shown what we were. At the base of a tree that had been ripped from the ground by the recent tornado, we found something. It was small and garish and definitely out of place. I'll never forget it. It was a Native American fetish doll. Throughout Native American history, likenesses of animals were carved from stone. It was believed that these animal fetishes would aid a person or tribe in their time of need. But this was quite the opposite. This one was crafted to look human in shape, and it was made of branches and dried vines. The body was contorted and appeared to be in agony. To further accent this, it had thorny barbs protruding from its head. Unwilling to bind this object himself, John called in a local shaman to help out.

It was explained to us that this doll was created with the express purpose of bringing misfortune and harm to the intended target. There's the rub—it was created. Much like a voodoo doll, its existence was intentional. *Haunted Collector* was a show about helping people who might have haunted objects making life difficult for them. Haunted objects, as I've observed, generally fall into one of two categories. Category one: the item has energy associated with it, either inherently or due to a spirit that still has some affinity for it. Category two: the item is a catalyst for pre-existing energy at the location. When the item is brought in, its presence can activate dormant energy. In either case, the cause is energy. Energy, not intent. That's what made this item stand out to me. Someone's intent may have been controlling an energy—kind of like a curse. Perhaps curses were real after all.

This was not a random occurrence or the evolution of some other natural process. This was human evil at work. Someone made the doll, and someone placed it on the property. On our other cases, we'd identify the item and then remove it, calming things down for the people we'd come to help. But this time would be entirely different. No EMF meter I could wave around would detect the culprit. No gadget or amount of investigating the premises could reveal the maker's gripe for Tonie or the people at Jordan Springs. We would take the fetish doll away, but its creator was still out there, watching . . . waiting. Who knew if they would make another one or even elevate their methods? It was a sobering thought, but our job there was done: identifying and removing a paranormally hazardous object.

As far as a curse was concerned, the shaman did feel there was negative energy associated with both the doll and the land and that he would have to take steps to help clear it. At that moment, though, he wanted to be sure we were clear of any potential after-effects associated with it. So, to finalize our investigation, a closing ceremony was held. It was done in traditional Native American fashion, complete with a pipe and tobacco. The tobacco was meant as an offering to the spirits and to wish us a good journey on the road ahead.

The sun was going down over the horizon, painting the sky in an explosion of oranges, reds, and pinks. We stood outside the towering event center in a circle, the January breeze cool on our faces. The shaman lit the ceremonial pipe and passed it to John. In turn, we all took a pull, including Tonie. Then the wind ceased. The air was still, and the mood calm. The shaman spoke a few words and ended the formalities.

I was never a believer in such practices, but I do feel that something was accomplished with that ending ceremony. All the stress that had been building up in each of us over the past few weeks melted away. The frustration I felt about things behind the scenes had turned to gratitude. The snippiness that had been passing between some of us faded and revealed a stronger camaraderie. There was something else, too, something primal in the air. I felt like the world held endless possibilities again, and for a brief moment, I was reminded of my childhood. Apparently, Chris Zaffis felt it, too, for we both found ourselves wandering into the woods behind the event center. The others had gone back inside, but we wanted the adventure to continue. We explored the brook that wound into deeper woods and even took turns sitting on a tree stand we found attached to a massive oak. Few words were exchanged. The moment was too rare to muddle it with small talk or observation. What was in that pipe? You might be thinking. I don't know, but whatever it was, it had done its job.

If there had been a curse over Jordan Springs, I felt it had been lifted. All was right with the world, and as the moon rose through the cerulean sky, I knew that everything would be okay. I went to bed that night and had the best sleep I'd had in months.

12

The Black Cat Returns

In 2014, a storm of reports came out of the Vatican claiming that Pope Francis had made a momentous statement—animals had souls. "Paradise is open to all of God's creatures" was the quote that set the media landscape ablaze and caused animal lovers everywhere to rejoice. Finally, it seemed the Catholic Church had caught up to what the rest of us had known all along. Our pets, our faithful loved ones who are a part of our families, would go on after death, just as we do. We would see them again across The Rainbow Bridge. One only need gaze into the soulful eyes of their animal to believe it. They love us as much as we love them—how could there be any doubts?

Sadly, those reports were in error—at least about the source and the quote itself. Pope Francis never actually said those words as he addressed the gathering in St. Peter's Square. It turns out that something similar was spoken by Pope Paul VI decades ago. The exact words were, "One day, we will see our pets in the eternity of Christ." The current Pope had been speaking about a new interpretation of End Times, which was expanded upon by an Italian reporter. Pope Francis had made no such landmark statement. As quickly as we had it, we lost it—Papal legitimization of the existence of animal souls.

As skeptical a person as I can be, I've always believed that if we have souls, so must animals. It's the energy of life. Of course, that has always raised a score of questions about the topic. Questions no priest or pointy-hatted individual could ever clearly answer for me. Does the existence of animal souls extend to every branch of the animal kingdom? And if so, when we kill insects and other creatures we deem pests, are those considered murders that will impact our souls?

I've spoken to psychics who claim to commune with animal spirits. One such time, I dared to ask if they could reach out to my first pet, a cat named Smokey. I loved her but was sometimes too rough with her, and I've carried that guilt around for years. I wanted to see if contact could be made and if she might forgive me. The psychic attempted to find Smokey but couldn't, and she compared the experience to looking into a dark room. Of course, this explanation made me a little skeptical about the actuality of the psychic's gift. I nevertheless suggested another theory—perhaps my departed pet's soul was already in an alternate form and therefore inaccessible as her former identity. It was as good an explanation as any, I supposed.

Despite that skewed experience, I still maintained my belief in animal souls. Yes, it's an odd stance for me—blind belief or faith, you might call it. But that's what happens when we lose those we love. It's a consolation to believe—to hope—they still exist somewhere. I've lost acquaintances, college friends, associates, but never close family. I've yet to lose someone (a human) to death that causes me to hurt as deeply as if a part of me had died. I know that time is coming, just a normal part of life. It's not something I look forward to facing, but I am thankful that the following true story keeps the sputtering flame of faith alive for me.

***

"What should we name him? Salem? Sylvester? He's black, so those would be fitting," she suggested.

"It really doesn't matter; they respond to tone of voice, not language, specifically. You could name him anything, really," I responded casually.

I stood there in the store, shifting uncomfortably as I looked around. Stacked, stainless steel cages lined one side of the small room. Their furry cargo mewed and purred as children pointed while tugging on the pant legs of whichever parent was nearest. I glanced at each parent, noting the expressions of excitement mixed with panic. Clearly, none of them had intended to stop at the pet store that day, much less the adoption viewing room. I grinned inwardly, thinking how absurd it was to let a child call the shots when it came to taking on the responsibility of caring for a life.

That momentary wave of superiority vanished as I heard my girlfriend squeal in delight. I met the gaze of one of the fathers in the room—he flashed me an understanding smile. I, too, was one of those men powerless to say no to a loved one entranced by the awesome power of a meowing kitten. Against my earlier protestations that we didn't need an animal—especially in our tiny apartment—she had already selected an all-black specimen. He did not seem remarkable at all. Sitting neatly in his cage, looking out at the cacophony of dazzled humans, he simply stared. Not in the judgmental way some cats look while sizing you up. Nor with the pleading gaze of the animals you see in those commercials with sad Sarah McLachlan music. Neither of those described the demeanor of this kitten. He wasn't even acting cool, and he didn't seem to care if he was adopted or not. Had he been a device, you might've said he was in Power Save Mode.

But it was not this feline's lackluster behavior that roused me from my musings. Another kitten, this one black and white, had decided to put his two cents in about the situation. "ME-OW!" he demanded while sticking a paw between the bars. *Excuse me; I'm right here*, spoke his body language. He shifted back and forth expectantly as Nikki approached. A bundle of personality, this one was. He was reeling her in as I watched in slow motion, and the sounds around me faded. The black cat in the cage below him continued to stare. Then, he looked up at me. His expression did not change, but I knew then and there we were going home with two cats.

***

"Can you go grab Salem? It's time to give him his hairball stuff," she asked.

"Did you mean beadie, or beadie?" I inquired.

"They have names, you know."

"We've been through this before. You can call them whatever you want as long as it's in the right tone of voice. You feed them; you clean their litter; you are essentially their slave. That's why I call all cats "beadies." It's as arbitrary as any other name. Watch this. . ."

I made some psst sounds as I called out for the cat. I waited.

It had been several years since I'd owned a cat. When I was ten years old, I remember spending many days wandering around the Staten Island Mall while my mother was at work. She waitressed at a restaurant that specialized in ice cream sundaes, and during the summer, she often took me to work with her. I'd sit in the backroom and try to entertain myself with whatever a ten-year-old finds interesting. There was only so much small talk from my mother's co-workers that either party could stand, so I usually walked around and window shopped. Most of the places were boring for a young boy—clothing stores, appliance outlets, more clothing stores—not a single comic shop in the whole complex! As a result, much of my time was spent browsing the toy store and visiting the pet shop.

One of those summer days, I found myself enamored with a grey and white kitten I'd seen in the front window. For a child, killing time on an adult's work schedule, a 9-5 shift felt like a year. So, for that 365-day-eight-hour period, I bonded through the glass with a cat I would shortly bring home and name Smokey. I would have her for ten years before cancer forced us to put her to sleep. I held her as the veterinarian administered the injection. My mother held me as we both wept, and my world fell apart. In the years that followed, a part of me hardened. Determined never to feel such pain again, I closed myself off to ever having another pet.

And so I waited. I waited for this cat with which I had no connection, one that I called by the generic name "beadie." The two cats had joined our household several months ago. I found them pleasant enough, but I made the clear distinction that they were her cats, and their feeding and care were her responsibility.

The black and white feline was clearly dominant. I'd watch him run around, getting into trouble, knocking things off shelves, opening cabinets to grab food, sneak attacking his "little brother," and other such things. He enjoyed playing with Nikki and the toys she would buy them. He was a dynamo of energy—your all-around rambunctious young cat. The all-black one was quite the opposite. He usually just stared. He was aloof and quiet. We'd often wondered if he had something wrong upstairs—a wire loose or something. They had different and unique personalities. True, I'd gotten to know them better as we shared a living space, but I didn't feel ownership of either of them. Their designations remained uniform and lower case.

I called out one more time. Then the one Nikki had named Salem poked his head out from under an end table, his soulful eyes locking with mine.

***

We can do nothing to stop time's ever-forward march, and it seems equally futile to try and delay change. And so it was that I found myself alone in the apartment I once shared with Nikki and her two cats. Well, almost alone. Our time together had ended, and when she left, Nikki took what she could carry and said she'd be back for the rest. But her exodus resulted in the two cats being separated.

"I'll be back for Salem," she promised.

"We'll be here," I replied.

She may have given him a name, but I never recognized it. It lacked imagination. It lacked originality. By this time, I respected this animal too much to trivialize his existence with a name that was tied to his fur color. I've always wondered: Does a name shape the personality one becomes, or is one named for their inherent qualities? She gave him a name, but she never returned for him.

Over the weeks and months that followed, I saw a definite change in the cat. Without his older, obnoxious brother picking on him, he was able to come into his own. With the Alpha gone, he was able to ascend and be his self. He walked more proudly, he played, he jumped, and he meowed. He saw me. When he looked at me, he saw me as an individual. He knew me. And I finally allowed myself to see him and know him. No longer was he beadie with a lower case 'b.'

His name was Beadie.

The years were happy ones. Whenever I'd come home, he would meow loudly and impatiently, as if demanding to know why I'd been gone so long. He would sleep at the foot of my bed at night. He would lie on his back on the floor, contently basking in the summer sun. In the winter, he preferred his spot on the back of the couch. We had our routines. He knew when I was upset. He knew when I was happy. At any time, I could call out, "Where's that Beadie?" and wherever he was, I would hear his meow. When I sat at the computer, I would often feel a paw on my thigh. Looking down, I could see he wanted to come and sit on my lap as I worked. As a result of this, many of my video projects would have "B.D. Editing" included in the credits as a nod to this animal who would never see it but who was such a part of me that his inclusion was mandatory.

Such gestures were not one-sided by any means. I never imagined a cat could make for such an effective wingman. Being newly single and back in the sometimes confusing and awkward dating scene, I occasionally brought company back to the apartment. Beadie would come out to evaluate my choice of date. Being who I am, I would not mesh well with anyone who did not love animals, so that was never an issue. They would see him and say, "What a sweetheart! Come up here, cutie!" He would then play the part of the curious cat, hopping up on the couch and sniffing and inspecting while being petted. Arching his back and purring, he created a mood. Looking up at my company and then at me, if he could wink, I believe he would have. The hand of my visiting friend still stroking his fur, he then would walk from her lap to mine, being sure to deliver that physical attention my way. He'd always linger for a moment to be sure everything was proceeding smoothly; then, he'd take his leave and go about his own business as nature took its course.

He was my best friend. Talking about him made me smile. When people would ask how he got his name, I'd explain how all cats were generically "beadies," but he was special—he got a capital "B." Additionally, his name was also an adjective, as I would often say he was being beadie, as well as being the beadiest of all beadies.

Once again, I owned a pet. I was happy to take on the responsibilities that it entailed. But more than that, I had a friend. One who loved unconditionally, beyond the limited assumptions with which I had armored myself over the years. Deep down, I knew I had been hiding—not wanting to reopen my heart to potential pain. But Beadie had become a part of me. When I was doing well, he thrived. When he was sick, I felt sick. Everything I am today, he witnessed me become. He was a part of that transformation, and I could not imagine, nor did I want to, my life without him.

***

I was on the road filming *Haunted Collector* when Beadie got sick. I remember pacing the lobby of a resort in Ohio while on hold with the vet, awaiting blood test results. I was on an adventure that many coveted, and all I wanted to do was go home and be sure my cat was okay. After an agonizing wait, I was informed Beadie had a thyroid problem that could be regulated with pills, but otherwise, he would be okay. I was thankful there was something that could be done, but it planted the seed in my mind. A dark, terrifying realization came to me, an obvious one that no pet owner ever wants to confront . . . our time was running out. Being in the paranormal, I reached out to energy workers and reiki masters, hoping to do what I could to extend that time. The thought often crossed my mind that if I could sacrifice years of my own to buy him more time, I'd forfeit them gladly. Such is love.

Could my work in the paranormal offer me some solution? Would my understanding of an afterlife grant me a reward of exception? The byline on a slow news day would be "OLDEST CAT CONFIRMED: 35 YEARS AND COUNTING" with a picture of Beadie and me relaxing together as we often did. It was a foolish hope, but as the years elapsed, I dared to hope all the same. Yet, the dark thoughts never left me. I always wondered if today would be the day I'd come home to find him . . .

One upshot to my television show being discontinued was the chance to be home more. In the final days, Beadie and I did our best to carry on as things had been, albeit a slower version. His fur wasn't as shiny, the flaky bits were constant, and the litter box was missed more often than not, but I took each day as a gift and greedily hoped for another. When I'd come home, I would scoop him up and hold him across my shoulder as I always did, and he would purr. I'd have been content to stay in that moment forever.

***

Our last day was October 5th. The details will never be purged from my memory, but I choose not to immortalize certain ones in print.

"I'm so sorry. You can take as much time as you need, and I'll come back in when you're ready," the vet tech apologized.

I could barely croak out a response.

I held my best friend in my lap. He was scared and confused. I was distraught. The animal I had not wanted to take home a lifetime ago, I could now not let go. The tragedy of a terminal situation is choice. We, as caretakers, are given the choice to hang on or let go. We have to make the decision, and then we must live with it.

Time stood still in the room that day. The minute details remain irrevocably carved into my mind. The smell of the cleaning products used on the examination table. The humming and beeping of nearby machines. The pale blue of the walls, broken only by the rack of care pamphlets, their distribution within the rack, their frazzled corners, the condition of each bit of paper. All is seared into my memory—nay, my worst nightmare. I had to give the order.

There was no movie montage of sunlight and happiness to precede the final moment. There was no orchestra to play him out—just a cruel silence—then nothing.

***

Life is a journey. It's not always easy. It shouldn't be, or it would not be worth living. I'm not a man of faith. I'm not a man who comes to belief easily. It took many trials and tribulations for me to get to where I am in the paranormal, in both a literal and figurative sense. I'd started my journey as a young boy who believed in everything. Then as I got older, I became jaded and cynical and shut out those things. As time went on, experiences opened those doors for me once again—slowly, deliberately, and with a message each time.

I left the animal hospital with only a postcard containing Beadie's name and paw prints. That was all I had to show for 16 years. So tragically unfair. I felt robbed, cheated—even my work in the paranormal wasn't enough to allow me to believe that the spirit of my friend would live on.

That is until his ashes arrived home a week later.

They were contained in a simple yet tasteful wooden box with a brass placard that read "Beadie." I placed it on a shelf and put his favorite toy next to it. The week had been a tough one. I still hadn't quite processed what had happened, and this once again made it real. I went to bed that night with the wound freshly gouged, and then…

I sit on what I recognize as my bed. My back is against the wall. Whatever I'd intended on doing next is interrupted by a vibration. Something has jumped up on the bed with me. It only takes a moment to recognize whom. I see his black fur, shiny and healthy. His eyes are golden and clear. I hear him purring loudly and strongly. Beadie walks across the bed and curls himself into the crook of my arm, as he used to always do on the couch. As he sits there, he looks back at me like old times. His purr is so loud it wakes me like a splash of water to the face . . .

I bolted straight up in the sheets. Looking around, I searched for signs of which reality I was in—the clock on the night table read 3:15

am. I'm not a believer in the 3:00 am phenomenon, when the veil between worlds is said to be at its thinnest, but the dream had been so vivid, so real, that I had to take note of the time. I stumbled out of bed and into my living room, past Beadie's food and water dishes, past his scratching post, and straight to where the wooden box sat.

I believe Beadie came to visit me that night. In those moments, he came to let me know he still exists beyond just my memories of him. His soul—his energy—is still out there. He came to reaffirm my faith, to keep me from retreating into a fortress of walls and cynicism. Love is forever. Despite the pain I feel over his absence, knowing that his essence is eternal does soothe the loss. I hope to see him again someday.

* An earlier version of this story was published in *Tails from the Other Side: Pets & the Paranormal* (Myth Ink Books, 2016), with all proceeds supporting animal rescue.

13

Suggested Reading

Being on the road shooting *Haunted Collector*, doing case after case with John Zaffis and the family, was the adventure of a lifetime. Season one was a learning curve as we saw the daily ins and outs of producing a network TV show. I'd done my own documentaries in the past, so I had minor insight, but John didn't understand the workflow at first. At the end of each day that first season, we'd walk across the street from our hotel to Burger King and just blow off steam. That became our tradition. I was baffled by the network's notes regarding the team and how we would be portrayed.

"That's just how producers are, kiddo," John would say. Then he'd sip his coffee and complain about them making us record so many takes of an OTF or a walk-up to a location.

"That's just how production works," I'd reply.

We both had pieces of this strange new puzzle, and we were figuring it out together.

I'm a wanderer at heart. I love traveling to new places and seeing new things. The allure of the road was intoxicating for me. A new town, a new hotel, finding a place to eat where the locals would welcome you and share their stories—all of these things added to the adventure of filming a television show about investigating the paranormal.

Rolling into an unfamiliar town brought with it a routine. Typically, I would be the one driving the van. John would sit in the passenger seat, and Chris, Aimee, and Beth would fill the back. After Beth left the show, Jason and Jesslyn would take residence back there. Pulling up to our temporary home for the week, the denizens of the rental van would wake up and disembark. After being processed by the front desk, we would shuffle off to our rooms, comparing notes as we walked.

"What room are you in?"

"I need to go to Walmart to pick up . . ."

"Think my room will have a hot tub again?"

The routine would continue. We'd all get to our rooms, freshen up a bit, and make ourselves at home. For those of us in close proximity, we'd duck our heads into each other's rooms to see who had gotten the best one. Often, the girls would plan out their evenings while the boys ventured out to Walmart to procure snacks. That, too, always went the same. Badger (my nickname for Chris Zaffis), Jason, and I would each grab a shopping cart and disperse throughout the aisles. When we reconvened, we'd compare items. Badger and I would marvel at the healthy things Jay had assembled: a gallon of milk, a bunch of bananas, some granola bars. I was shocked the one time he selected a rather large summer sausage! In Badger's cart was always a six-pack of Yuengling beer, Bagel Bites, and some Slim Jims. Dr. Pepper and Chili Cheese Fritos were my staples.

Don't get me wrong, the retelling of these routines might make the whole thing sound mundane, but we all found it quite comforting. It was the constant in our ever-changing reality, and it served to ground us.

Grounding was definitely needed since we were going from case to case at such a rapid pace. It was fun, an adventure, but it was not a vacation—we were there to do a job. With that in mind, I was always eager to get to the location as soon as possible to do a walkthrough. To look around and get a feel for what we were getting into. *Haunted Collector* was about a family of investigators (both literally and figuratively) helping other families in need. The events seen on the show were only the tip of the iceberg. There was so much seen and experienced by both the cast and crew that unfortunately never made it to the audience. Like this never-aired experience from our investigation at Browse Awhile Books in Tipp City, OH.

***

Browse Awhile Books was a quaint, populous used bookstore. The main area was filled with a variety of old books, including two large bookcases of paranormal titles. Shelves of books filled a hallway that led to the rear of the store, where another room was packed with written volumes. Two smaller rooms off the hallway housed even more books. In the back room was a staircase that led to the basement, which was almost completely full of, you guessed it, more books.

The production crew was busy setting up the area and figuring out logistics. The cast had arrived to film the in-van approach and John and Aimee's walkthrough. We had learned that the back room was the sci-fi section, so Badger and I decided to check it out. I liked perusing bookstores to see what *Star Trek* and *Dragonlance* titles were in stock. As we made our way through the store, we were greeted by a few producers and a camera guy. I'd soon be greeted by someone (or something) else as well.

Walking down the narrow hallway towards the back, a book suddenly flew off a nearby shelf and landed at my feet! Startled, I turned around to look at Badger.

"You saw that, right?" I asked. He nodded in the affirmative.

I turned back to look at the book on the floor and the shelf it had come from. It didn't come from a poorly balanced stack of books. There was also no room for it to have just been perched on the edge, waiting for a vibration that would allow gravity to take over. Everything on the shelf was perfectly in place. This book was thrown with force. Both of us examined the shelf and then glanced at each other.

"Yep," he began, "same as it ever was."

Picking up the book, I noticed it was one about World War II fighter planes. I'd always been an aficionado of that era's aircraft, and it's a dream of mine to fly one someday. Could this be a coincidence, or was the store introducing itself to me with a reading suggestion it thought I would enjoy? We both chuckled as we continued to the back room.

This case would be an interesting one for sure since the activity had already begun, and the cameras weren't even rolling yet. On *Haunted Collector*, as with *SCARED!,* I served as the scientist—the guy who looked for the logical explanation of things. As John said in the opening titles, "Brian, my tech guy . . .," I would approach every investigation with all the tools and toys at my disposal. But this personal experience—a book thrown at my feet—was a valid one despite not being recorded. It was part of the whole story. As I've already noted in previous chapters, investigations are not just about the EVPs and EMF variances measured. They're equally—sometimes more so—about personal experiences. I've always said that spirits don't appear on cue. The ones at Browse Awhile Books were greeting us on their own time, and I'm glad I was open enough to recognize it.

Such experiences can attach you to a place, I've found. I've been back there many times since the episode was filmed. A visit to Browse Awhile Books now has a routine of its own for me. I show up, buy a bunch of paranormal titles, have lunch with the staff, and then hang out for a little bit. They have become good friends. I think the spirits approve as well, although it's been some time since they've recommended a book. Maybe next visit.

14

Hooked on a Feeling

One common trope of The Work is that the longer you do it, the more in tune you become to the energies around you. It takes time and patience but given enough experience; you will develop a heightened sensitivity. It's different for each person, of course, and the areas of development vary.

Our bodies are amazing machines, capable of many different functions, most of which operate in the background. Consider for a moment all the things your body is doing right now. Your eyes are scanning this page, poring over the written words, while your brain is reconciling symbols to the translation matrix therein that understands what they mean. As you do this, you are drawing breath. You are exhaling. The blood pumping through your veins delivers oxygen to the various organs in your body, which in turn are busy working on their specific tasks. If you ate recently, your digestive system is breaking that food down into energy. Your body temperature is being maintained. On a microscopic level, new skin cells are being formed as old ones die. Your hair and nails are growing (hair at a rate of .0178 inches a day). Your body is an amazing machine—but I said that already, didn't I?

Let's not forget the intangibles—the things that cannot be measured on any definitive scale. Emotions, desires, ambitions, intuition; these are the things that color our personalities and define who we are. But how does this all work? Can one be who they are in a vacuum?

We are equipped with senses to take in information from the environment around us. The classic five senses we use daily: sight, hearing, taste, smell, and touch. The oft-debated sixth sense, your psychic ability or third eye, is one that we all have, but many do not access it. Those who do, don't use it every waking moment. The same could be said of the other five senses. You're not always smelling or touching or paying attention to every sound you hear. So, following that logic, your sixth sense also comes into play when it is needed. But when exactly is that? Psychic ability is something I suspect has atrophied in our species over time. Much like when I joke about a seventh sense—common sense. If you don't use it, you begin to lose it.

Senses are complicated functions. They originate from the physical. Take your eyes, for instance; they are complex instruments that have many parts working in concert to deliver something we take for granted—sight. We see the world around us in high definition, in color, and varying conditions.

Every sense contributes to our conscious experience, and most often, we pay no attention to the inner workings that go into the weaving of that tapestry. They operate like a movie crew. If you sit and watch the credits roll, you'll see the names of numerous people that worked on the film. Each one had a task to perform, and the collective result was a complete cinematic experience. Sure, the director and the actors get all the accolades, but none of it would have been possible without the foley artist, the gaffer, the key grip, and many, many others. Your life is a movie, and there are many processes at work behind the scenes to make that life as brilliant to behold as possible.

But where does your psychic ability fit in? Furthermore, what exactly does it entail? That's the complicated part. To date, psychic ability has not been sufficiently proven by science. Parapsychology does its best to analyze and investigate claims of psychic ability, but sadly, it is not considered a respected avenue of study by the general academic community.

I've met many people who claim to be psychic. Their particular areas of sensitivity are as diverse as the job descriptions from our movie analogy. Some are mediums who speak to spirits, while others practice psychometry, which is the reading of energy from objects. Many psychics feel they are adept with extrasensory perception, using either precognition or retrocognition. I've seen the clairvoyant kind working with law enforcement to locate missing people. Whenever I'm feeling ill, there are scores of psychics who offer to send me reiki. The list goes on and on, but the one term that strikes a chord within me is empath.

The Merriam-Webster Dictionary defines empathy as: "The action of understanding, being aware of, being sensitive to, and vicariously experiencing the feelings, thoughts, and experience of another of either the past or present without having the feelings, thoughts, and experience fully communicated in an objectively explicit manner."

Most people feel empathy; it's part of being human. When you watch a skateboarding video and cringe as the skater wipes out fantastically, that is empathy. The revelation of a horrendous wound at the end usually brings further emotion, typically sympathy. The two are closely related but not the same. Sympathy would be to feel sadness or worry for the skater and his ordeal; empathy would be the personalization of it—feeling what he feels within yourself.

Bringing up movies again, the ones that mean the most to us are the ones that trigger our empathic response. Personally connecting or identifying with a character's feelings or narrative is what makes a movie engaging to the viewer. That's why triumphs in a film are so satisfying. You don't have to be a boxer to revel with Rocky Balboa. His cry of "Yo, Adrian, I did it!" has echoed in all of us at some time or another.

This is how most of us experience empathy. It's a difficult state to process since it happens all within the mind, but there is a deeper potential there. As I said, most can experience empathy, but psychic empathy is something else.

An empath has the ability to sense and feel the emotional states of others without being shown or told anything about them. This makes them a sponge to the energies of people around them. It's not uncommon for an empath to feel how those around them do and not know why. That's what made the term stick out to me. It seemed to explain something about myself. It sheds light on an area in which I was often confused.

I would notice it when walking around Manhattan. I'd pass a building or an alleyway and see something that would trigger a deep and sudden emotion within me. Because these locations were not connected to any personal memory, I'd often wonder why I felt such sadness or elation. In a city the size of New York, the number of people leaving behind impressions is innumerable, and most impressions passed as quickly as they came to me. They were elements of the environment, not a direct stream of information. The latter, I found, was something different and much harder to shake off.

In my social groups, I'm often the person people talk to about their problems. I'm a good listener, so I listen. Sometimes I give advice, but I generally take on a passive role and let them talk. Whatever the problem, no matter how big or small, I've always made time to help out a friend in need. Now, when I say help out, I'm not talking about giving lifts to the airport or helping them move. I'm talking about helping them process life struggles, the issues that give us pause and make us seek counsel. If a friend was thinking about changing jobs and unsure of what to do, I listened. If a friend was having trouble with their significant other, I would sit back and listen. Whatever the topic, the doctor was in. I took a certain pride in doing so as if I were helping just by being there, which was true in most cases since having a safe place to vent is an important part of dealing with problems. Psychology was one of my areas of study in school, and the workings of the mind and how people behave were fascinating to me. I would often joke that I should start charging by the hour and get a proper couch for the practice.

After disclosing details and exploring scenarios, my friends would often say they felt lighter and more able to deal with the issue at hand. I, however, had a different experience. As happy as I was to help out, I often noticed that I felt encumbered, sluggish, and burdened afterward. As if the problems I had listened to were now my own. Why was this happening?

I usually chalked it up to being tired from work, an impending cold, or some other explanation. I never even considered the transference of emotional energy, but that's what was occurring. I was soaking it up but not wringing it back out. This went on for years and began to take a toll on me. I found myself growing more cynical, more impatient. Unbeknownst to me at the time, all those negative experiences were getting cataloged into my personal worldview.

At this point in the telling, I pause to consider an alternative explanation. The world can be a crazy place. It's full of challenges and obstacles, and if you're not careful, it will beat you into submission. I was in my late twenties, I had just gotten out of college, and working in Manhattan. The commute was long; the job was taxing. Then, 9/11 happened, and we found ourselves in a war every other week.

The War on Terror, the War on Drugs—conflict became a constant companion that was with us every waking hour, to the point that it felt odd if we were not fighting something. I developed a besieged mentality as if everyone and everything was out to get me. The stresses of modern life are prime candidates to push one into the cynical end of the pool.

But looking back now, I see that this feeling of being burdened did not originate in my twenties, nor did it seem pinned to any one event or time period. I was always a sensitive person. I recall being a little boy sitting on the couch with my parents as we watched a nature documentary. I cried because a gazelle was unable to escape a predatory lion's jaws. As the likely voice of Sir David Attenborough described the scene, I asked why this had to happen. Why was nature so seemingly unfair? My parents gently explained to me how Nature had to provide for the lion as well as the gazelle and that there was a balance.

Years later, I endured many sleepless nights in my room as I panicked over the state of the world. The threat of nuclear war always seemed just on the other side of the door. The TV movie *The Day After* and growing tensions with the Soviet Union did nothing to calm those fears. In a most Pavlovian manner, those feelings of dread re-manifest any time I hear Sting's "Russians" and the lyrics: "Believe me when I say to you, I hope the Russians love their children too . . ."

More time passed, and the geopolitical tension of the Cold War eased. Yet, as these old adversaries seemed less and less threatening, new ones rose to take their place. I vividly remember the concern in my mother's voice when she came into my room to tell me that missiles had been fired into Kuwait and war had begun. What became known as Operation Desert Shield and later the Gulf War was my introduction to the seemingly never-ending conflict in that region of the world. I failed to see Nature's balance in it all. If anything, it appeared to be a pendulum that swung between different nations and persons but delivered the same result every time.

I had recently discovered the writings of Nostradamus and the many interpretations of his alleged predictions. My anxious nature at the time made every quatrain seem as if it were a cosmic blueprint accurately detailing past events as well as those yet to come. The future no longer looked bright, but it seemed so clear what needed to be done. John Lennon wasn't wrong—give peace a chance! I felt as if the Universe were delivering me all the required information. In my muddled musings in my room at night, I would think to myself that if I could somehow write a heartfelt, convincing letter to the President or to the United Nations, they would have to listen. What would be the point of forecasting world events if they couldn't be averted? I doubted that Nostradamus would have done it just for kicks or to impress his friends at parties. How many other people before him had tried to steer the ship away from the brink? I felt so strongly about all of it, but I never questioned where my feelings were coming from. I did doubt them, however. I felt I'd be a modern-day Cassandra, with knowledge of the future but unable to do anything to change it.

That may have been the first stage of me attempting to cope with my empathic nature. I don't remember exactly when or what triggered it, but I began to shut down my psychic empathy at some point. The daily panic was just too much. It was a herculean task, carrying around the weight of the world on my shoulders, a burden no one asked of me. A burden I kept to myself.

But was I the only one feeling that way? I assumed so but analyzing it with the knowledge and experience I now have, maybe I was wrong. From my childhood perspective, my parents were strong and wise and had all the answers. I would never have imagined they had troubles or concerns. Now, I have insight into the worries an adult carries. Maybe my burgeoning ability had me soaking up their fear of a tumultuous world and their attempt to shield me from the darker parts of it.

Now don't get me wrong: I had an idyllic childhood despite this admission of near-daily panic. Fuzzy memories of Sunday drives, Little League, piano lessons, and Cub Scouts color my Kodachrome recollections. All made possible by my parents. They were the unsung crew of my movie. I experienced joy and stability because of their struggles and sacrifices. Perhaps therein lay the balance they spoke of. Sometimes you're the lion; sometimes, you're the gazelle. This was true of them, and I still carry some shame for not realizing it sooner. Like today, I had empathic ability in my youth but failed back then to recognize hurts and fears in those closest to me, dwelling instead upon my own.

I grew jaded and skeptical as if the denial of everything could nullify the future's unpleasant elements. To say I was moody was an understatement! But I feared no more for the fate of the world.

Thoughts of Armageddon no longer plagued my slumber. It was a tenuous peace, though, for the colors of life had faded to shades of grey. The possibility of accepting my empathic nature was nil. I had armored myself against the slings and arrows of outrageous fortune, and in doing so, walled off that part of me, at least my awareness of it. The ability was still operating under the surface, on a very local level.

But just as that wall in Berlin came down, so did my own, just not as quickly. My exploration of the paranormal helped dismantle it gradually, brick by brick, piece by piece. Light made its way through cracks in the mortar. Sections that had been attacked and clawed let in air from the outside, dispelling the stagnation within. Having emerged from this figurative bunker, I see it now as an obsolete relic from a war without beginning or end. The conflict is existence, and I'd sought to remove myself from the particulars of it. My own enterprises of great pitch and moment had lost the name of action while I remained behind those walls.

I have reluctantly accepted this about myself—I am empathic. Not just because the final scene of *The Green Mile* always brings me to tears, but because I am sensitive to the energies of others and must be vigilant not to let them affect me or, worse, internalize them as my own. That has been the greatest challenge so far: discerning my emotions from those of others. I've also begun to experience what I call "tremors," in which I find myself in a concentrated state of anxiety just before a negative occurrence. The occurrence itself could be a phone call with bad news, a stroke of misfortune, or a physical malady. The recognition of the event serves to validate the tremor, and it's happened enough that I'm now bothered when I feel a tremor coming on. Yes, I lifted the term from *Star Wars*, where Obi-Wan felt a "tremor in the Force." If I'm going to be stuck with emotional abilities, I'm determined to have some fun with them, damn it! I have yet to recognize the opposite—a positive counterpart to the negative tremor. My natural cynicism makes it difficult to identify, if I even have one at all.

Speaking in this manner—saying I have an ability beyond something tangible—still makes me uncomfortable, like wearing an ill-fitting outfit. I don't want to draw attention to myself as an empath, yet here I am writing about it, forcing myself to embrace the very thing I routinely tell audiences: Psychics are not superheroes. They do not have superhuman abilities, nor are they infallible.

The large variation in psychic abilities remains greatly misunderstood, and I try to explain it with this example: Imagine you are stuck in standstill traffic. As you sit in your car, you wonder what could be causing the hold-up. You look around and see other stopped vehicles, with other drivers glancing about. Opening the car door and getting out, you look down the road. You see more cars and a bend in the road ahead. Beyond that, you cannot see. That is what the average person experiences every day of their life—a journey whose outcome is unknown. We are all traveling down that figurative road.

Now, on the side of that same road is a cell phone tower. Working at the top is a field technician. They look down and notice the traffic has stopped for miles in both directions. But the technician has a better vantage point than the motorists on the ground. From the tower, they can see past the bend in the highway to where an accident has occurred. The details are a bit fuzzy, but the lights from the emergency vehicles can be seen clearly, as can the tow truck, making its way to the crash on the median. Below, someone asks what's going on, and the technician shouts down what they see. This is how it is for psychics in general. They are not magical; they just have better vantage points, giving them access to more information. To further hammer down that point, they, too, are utilizing *all* of their senses, which means they are operating with the same inputs as the rest of the population. They can be wrong.

"Your eyes can deceive you. Don't trust them," instructed Obi-Wan to Luke. Did you think I was done with the *Star Wars* references? Surely not! This piece of advice from a sci-fi film holds true in real life. Our senses are fallible, and as we get older, they become less and less reliable. Our eyesight blurs, our hearing becomes muffled, maladies later in life can rob us of our ability to feel via touch. We've all experienced a temporary loss of taste when we have a cold. So how can we put so much reliance on our senses when it's proven they cannot always be trusted?

I began this chapter by saying that our bodies are amazing machines. I also said that as you do The Work, your sensitivity will increase over time. Experience is a wonderful teacher. So, as we age, our senses may dull, but perhaps, our feelings compensate.

"Stretch out with your feelings . . ." Obi-Wan instructed. Later on, both he and Vader ordered Luke to search his feelings to discover the truth—another nugget of wisdom hidden within this infamous space opera. The Jedi used empathic ability to gain information and influence the weak-minded. Naturally, as a child, I wanted to be Luke Skywalker, have a lightsaber, and pilot an X-Wing fighter. I even tried to move things in my room using The Force more times than I could count (with a 100% failure rate)! So, here I am in adulthood, accepting my empathic potential and stretching out with my feelings. Brian J. Cano, Jedi Knight!

In all seriousness, identifying as an empath has been quite a realization. I continue to explore what it means for me and humankind in general. I still have many questions, but the walls are down, and I remain watchful. The world is still a crazy scary place. The fears and dangers are ever-present; only their names have changed. Ayatollah Khomeini is now Kim Jong Un. Nuclear Armageddon is now the zombie apocalypse. We always seem to be hovering on the brink of annihilation.

However, while I can acknowledge the dark side of existence, I won't forget to maintain balance in my life, and neither should you. Every moment of fear and uncertainty can be offset by a beautiful sunset or a moving piece of music. It's an ongoing struggle, but that's life, right? And if, via my empathy, I can help others find their moments of bliss, then as before: the doctor is in.

15

Two Steps Forward

Driving home from a visit with my parents, I noticed the old, abandoned gypsum plant on the edge of Richmond Terrace had been torn down. The sprawling complex that had dominated the waterfront property was gone. The towering silos, the imposing walls, the network of walkways connecting the sections— vanished. I could now clearly see the water and the industrial buildings across the reach in Bayonne. The change of view was fascinating to me—I had gotten so accustomed to that building being there that I never considered what was on the other side—but also a bit of a shock.

I'd had some of my first childhood adventures in that abandoned gypsum plant. I would go urban exploring in its many halls, rooms, and gantry ways. For me, it was a fortress to explore or an enemy stronghold I must infiltrate. Sometimes it was the ruins of a crashed spaceship. Other times it was the remains of a long-dead civilization. In the early Eighties, my imagination dressed it with whatever facade seemed appropriate for that day. It was an abandoned building in a rough area of Staten Island, but my young mind did not grasp the dangers inherent in such a place. I was fearless back then . . . or oblivious. My first official foray into the paranormal was still more than a decade in the future, but perhaps some of my training for it happened here.

In those days, the hours stretched to infinity as I explored the place. Getting inside was easy; there were plenty of access points, be it a ruined wall or an old door rusted ajar. I felt like Indiana Jones, spelunking into an overgrown temple, looking for traps, and searching out treasure. I'd roamed the massive rooms and tunnels often, so I had a mental map of the place. One of my favorite activities was climbing up onto the towers and gantry ways that reached high up between silos. I found it desolate yet peaceful. I'd often bring a sandwich from the local deli and pick a spot to eat lunch somewhere up high, so I could survey the entire island or watch the boats go by. It was almost as if this place were meant for me and stayed abandoned so I could continue my adventures within it. It used to be the home of U.S. Gypsum, which made fireproof sheetrock, plaster, and paint. I didn't know what any of that was at the time, but I can still remember how the sun would paint the walls and floor as it shone through breaches in the ceiling. Old, ruined machinery inhabited the rooms and added to my mental set dressing.

Did the building know me? As I got to know it, did it welcome me when I would return each time? I felt comfortable there, so I had no reason to think otherwise. No flag had been planted, but I did feel like I had claimed it, made it my domain. That is, until one day, many adventures later.

The hour was late, and the setting sun cast long shadows in the soft, orange glow of the chamber. One of the grand hangar-like rooms on the first level had several smaller alcoves jutting off it. The smaller rooms became caves, dark and spooky. As I passed one, in particular, I noticed something I hadn't seen in prior visits—a massive, concrete block had been situated near the entrance to one of the cave-like offshoots. I couldn't see anything in the murky darkness ahead but laid out neatly on the block was a pair of white socks. I froze in my tracks.

Naturally, I wasn't afraid of the footwear but rather what it implied. They weren't dirty or burned or thrown haphazardly on the floor. They had been purposely placed on the block, perhaps to dry in the earlier day's sun. And inside that darkness may have been the owner of the socks. A homeless person. Possibly a dangerous one. In our modern mentality, one might think: *You don't know their story. It's wrong to assume they'd be dangerous just because they've fallen on hard times.* But in the mind of an eleven-year-old who assumed he had the complex to himself, discovering that he may not be alone set off a red flag. My sense of adventure quelled for the day; I immediately made haste to exit.

I never saw to whom those socks belonged, nor did I ever encounter another human being in there, but I explored that building less and less as the weeks went on and steered clear of that section when I did. The seed of fear had been planted. I wasn't Indiana Jones. My domain had been invaded.

As I grew older and the summers grew shorter, and the years elapsed quicker, I still had many adventures in and around my neighborhood. A place called Snug Harbor comes to mind. Today it is a cultural center that often serves as a set piece for many Hollywood film and TV productions. Back then, it was a struggling tract of land that tried to find its identity after having been a place where old and decrepit sailors would go to live out their remaining days. The sailors were long gone, and many of the buildings had become abandoned and ruined. I'd explored many of them on several occasions. On one particular occasion, I found myself in what is now an administration building (then a decaying mansion). As I wandered the first floor, I heard a sound above me. I wasn't sure what it was—it wasn't a moan, it wasn't a scream, but it sounded anguished. No bird or animal I knew of could produce such a sound, which had a certain sonic quality to it—as if it were coming from underground. I crept over to the bottom of the main staircase and peered up. It was a sunny, pleasant day. Dusty shafts of light pierced the walls, creating a kaleidoscope of color. I stood still, listening for whatever made the sound.

Just then, I felt a chill overpower me. I heard and saw nothing, but I felt as if I were being held against my will. Whatever was up there was going to come down the stairs at any moment and find me! I'd never experienced such a feeling. It was primal, something ancient. Raw fear was rushing through my veins, telling me to move quickly! Yet, I was still frozen in place. Still seeing nothing, I sensed something creeping closer to the top of the stairs. I had to get out of there! Finally, adrenaline surged past the fear and set me free! Turning around, I barreled through the foyer and out the window I had entered. I felt the unseen presence behind me while inside, but the moment the sun hit my back, I was safe. Not wanting to risk anything, I continued my retreat, running all the way home. That was perhaps my first encounter with something supernatural. Or maybe the first time I'd been aware of one.

In my solo *Stand By Me* childhood, those two instances sowed the fear that would later be reaped during our taping of the first *Scared on Staten Island* episode.

***

The building commonly known as St. Augustine's Monastery was actually the Augustinian Academy, where boys were educated for the priesthood. It later became a retreat house that stood abandoned for years after a fire destroyed it. As with many such structures, the rumors and urban legends began to arise once it stopped being used. The alleged reports had gotten so widespread that it ended up as a piece in *Weird N.J.* issue #15 entitled, "Tales From an Abandoned Monastery on Staten Island." The article featured letters from people who had been there and related accounts of Satan worshippers, ghosts, and many, many sub levels. That last detail served as the centerpiece for a common rumor about a priest who murdered several of his students and entombed their bodies in the basement.

What seemed to anchor that story in my mind was one of the photos in the *Weird N.J.* spread. Among pictures of the dilapidated exterior and graffitied interior was a partial image of a room. The walls were covered from floor to ceiling with human skulls. Two robed figures stood guard, their heads bowed. The black and white picture covered less than a quarter page, but it may as well have been a mural in my mind.

Years had passed since my childhood adventures, and the routine of daily adult life had dulled those memories, but seeing this image reignited the feeling I had when I was young. I needed to find that room!

Before we'd set out to explore the place on camera, several scouting missions were made. These happened during the day and without any recording equipment. They also happened without me, as I had to work in the city while they were going on. I'll never forget those anxious afternoons spent in my editing bay at the ad agency, waiting for a call from the guys informing me they'd discovered the skull room. But the calls, when they came, were always disappointing.

"Did you find the room?" I'd ask.

"No, man, but we did find a door that should lead to the basement. It's boarded up, though," came the report. "We're going back tomorrow to see what else we can find."

Day after day, I'd answer the phone and listen to the ever-increasing progress, and yet, no skull room. And no network of sub levels. I didn't understand where the disconnect was. The article had run in a magazine—it was in print, and they couldn't print anything false, right? Oh, how naive I could sometimes be, despite my jaded nature.

So, it was looking like there would be no spooky room to discover, but we still had a project to complete and a complex to explore. Plans were set to return with our full crew, equipped with cameras we checked out from the local cable access station. Part of the fear we felt was the realization that if anything happened to those cameras while we were out there, we'd owe the station a pretty penny! Financial worries would soon give way to more primal ones.

It was a warm night on Grymes Hill—where St. Augustine's was located. The sounds of the highway below were masked by thick groves of trees and a persistent wind. I trampled through the forest with a camera rig perched on my shoulder. The light atop it shone like a beacon in the darkness. I was alone and looking like a lighthouse, visually announcing my presence to the creatures of the night.

Earlier that evening, we'd assembled in the main building and set up a base camp. After sorting through the tapes and wires and ensuring that everything was ready to go, we established challenges for ourselves. Someone would go into the bell tower and sit inside a pentagram. Someone would explore the lower levels in search of those elusive access points to the sub-basements. Someone brought a Ouija board along and would use it in the old chapel. Honestly, we didn't know what we were doing, but we thought these challenges would be entertaining. At the time, there was no *Ghost Hunters*, no

Ghost Adventures, nothing to compare to or imitate. We were pioneers in paranormal television, and we did the best we could.

My task was to locate the old basketball courts and investigate for signs of cult activity. We'd heard rumors that Satanists conducted rituals there. It was an outlandish thought—even more so now that I was stumbling about the woods looking for them!

I felt very exposed. If there was anyone else out there—especially the alleged cultists—I'd be in a dangerous predicament. The blinking red light on the camera indicated it was recording. I narrated every step I took, mindful to avoid any dead air. The visuals were shaky-cam footage of trees and rocks, so there had to be something underlying them to carry the scene. I know my droning wasn't the most informative or exciting, but it was real and honest. This was reality TV, after all—that's what the public wanted, right?

I was scared. You could hear it in my voice. At one point, I tried to comfort myself by just prattling on about the first thing that popped into my head. "Who am I? You sure you want to know? The story of my life is not for the faint of heart . . ." I crept down the overgrown path through the forest, reciting as much of the Spider-Man script as I could remember. So began my tradition of inserting movie quotes into almost every media appearance. I was even able to slip a lesser-known *Star Wars* quote into an episode of *Haunted Collector* since the famous quote from *Seven* kept getting identified and rejected. See if you can figure out which one—it's quite subtle.

This night on Grymes Hill, however, I wasn't quoting a movie to deliver a reference to the audience; I was truly trying to keep fear from overtaking me. It was all I could think of at the time. I was not a seasoned investigator but rather a rookie, green and inexperienced and out of my league for whatever I might encounter, be it ghosts, cultists, or worse. In all likelihood, I wouldn't come across any of those, but in my head at that moment, they were all waiting for me in the shadows, preparing to pounce when my guard was down. So I just kept talking, as if a pause in my tirade would allow the opening needed to attack. Such considerate adversaries! The illogic did not occur to me, so I rambled on.

Down the path I went, twisting through the trees and around the back of the property. It was a warm summer night, but the air held a chill, possibly caused by my mood. The moon above watched me with an unblinking stare, as it has at many a haunted location since.

It gazes, it records, it remembers—but this night, I was doing something new, instilling a fresh curiosity.

Eventually, I emerged from the woods into a clearing. Dirt and mud gave way to crumbling asphalt. The remnants of painted white lines on the ground revealed this to be the location I was searching for—the old basketball court. Clusters of trees and brush had claimed the area, regaling the few to find this spot with tales of years of abandonment. The metal rings upon which a net once hung were bare. The fence which had defined this area was long gone, survived only by a few rusty remnants of poles at the borders.

I felt a curious sensation as I stepped onto the court. It was as if the darkness was denser here, colder—as if I had stepped into a pool of water. My senses were on high alert. It was fear, raw and uncontrollable. In the woods, the trees had seemed to defend me, but now I felt those very same trees watching me from all around. All eyes in the forest were trained on me, an idiot with a camera and a bright light.

The first part of my objective had been completed—I'd found the courts. Now I had to do some investigating. My next goal was to find evidence of cult activity, whatever that entailed. Aside from actually walking in on a ceremony in progress, what could be considered a cult activity? Perhaps they left flyers lying around; "SACRIFICE THIS SATURDAY: One Night Only! Snacks Will Be Served! Bring Your Own Robe!"

Elsewhere on the property, the other team members were busy with missions of their own. Chris was trudging through a flooded basement corridor. Greg was sitting cross-legged up in the bell tower. Jason patrolled the front of the building. I thought of them and steeled myself to continue. I refused to be the weak link of the crew.

Part of our inspiration to do this was a show on MTV called *Fear*. It was a competition show where the channel's demographic would be dropped into allegedly haunted places and given dares to perform with the ultimate goal of winning prize money. The locations I would come to know very well in the near future, but at the time, they were all mysterious and far away. The contestants were not professional ghost hunters (a term which still belonged solely to Hans Holzer) and acted as producers loved to see them—scared and outrageous. One episode took place at a prison. A young man was required to spend time in solitary confinement (aka The Hole) by himself for twenty or so minutes. He went to the entrance of the area and just hung out. After the time had elapsed, he reported back to home base and told the others he'd done it. The imbecile must have forgotten he was on a reality television show and neglected to notice the stationary camera watching him from above. At the end of the episode, when the group expected to win and collect their money, it was revealed via the footage that his cowardice had denied them the victory.

Feeling frustrated, we raged at the seeming stupidity of the contestants and the fact that we could do nothing but shout at the screen. There was no real danger; this was a TV show! To be paid to sit alone in a room was child's play! The producers and the network wouldn't allow any harm to come to those kids. Signed waivers aside, no network wants the bad publicity of an accident or a death. We couldn't fathom why such a simple challenge was avoided. We vowed to get onto the show ourselves and show them how it was done.

Despite our viewership, we were just above the age bracket they were looking for, so we never made it onto *Fear*. Being denied that chance, we decided to do it ourselves, and *Scared on Staten Island* was born. Thanks, cowardly kid contestant! An interesting postscript to that memory happened when I began filming *Haunted Collector*. One of the executive producers for our show had also worked on MTV's *Fear*! We had a great conversation about how *Fear* had motivated and inspired me and landed me alone at St. Augustine's abandoned basketball courts, determined not to make the same faux pas as that kid assigned to solitary confinement. Looking back, I think I held my own on-screen, and I've continued to do so ever since, frustrating producers by showing little fear and no over-the-top reactions. Maybe that's why I've not gotten on another night-vision-heavy production. On that, I will continue to reflect. Meanwhile . . .

My novice self was questioning why he'd got off the couch to do this for real and discovering that fear was indeed a crippling emotion! But unlike the kid on *Fear*, I wasn't getting paid and had little to motivate me, save a dwindling resolve and the desire not to be made fun of for chickening out. I decided to simply focus on the task at hand—looking for signs that dark ceremonies had taken place there. Continuing to narrate for the audience, I did my best to sound official and informative. It's what we all do. I hear it even to this day, on all the shows. In place of experience or knowledge, one changes the way they speak to sound more authoritative. The prime example of this is the way we ask for a response. Instead of a simple "Hello, is there anyone here? Let me know if you are." That query filters through the paranormal stereotype database in one's head and comes out as, "If there are any spirits in here who wish to communicate, please make your presence known." Say it out loud. Go ahead; I'll wait. It might feel official at first, but if you listen to yourself, it sounds silly. Seriously, who talks like that? Aside from Mr. Spock and Egon Spengler, the average person does not string words together in that fashion. But when you begin investigating, to sound this way is the first step in fake it 'till you make it! I should know; I spoke those very words many times at the start of my paranormal journey.

Walking gingerly across the court, I kept my eyes focused on the ground. The cracks in the blacktop snaked in all directions, resembling the branches of a gnarled tree. Several areas had eroded away and formed small pits that appeared to have had fires recently set in them. No larger than my hand, they had remnants of ash around the sides. Traces of wax could be seen here and there in sloppy patterns. The white lines that had marked the point zones were nearly gone, but there was plenty of chalk graffiti around the area.

Near the pits were hastily drawn pentagrams. The ceremonial star within a circle was generally thought to be associated with black magic. The venerable pentacle was unknown to me at the time. I had yet to be introduced to Wicca and Earth Magick and all the variations therein. At that moment, the scrawled symbol was proof to me that something nefarious had gone down at this site.

My voice started to crack, and I began to stammer a word or two. I coughed and cleared my throat, trying to banish the growing dread. Purposely deepening my tone and still speaking in Official Voice Mode, I continued to report what I saw on my camera viewfinder. As was common in most abandoned places, plenty of red Solo cups indicated people had been drinking there recently. Maybe Satanists did offer refreshments at their rituals!

Looking more carefully at the graffiti on the ground, I tried to decipher the words in the rough script pattern. If they were indeed scrawled during a ceremony, it's possible that they were magical incantations used to summon or bind an entity. At least, that was what was running through my head. I zoomed in on one that wasn't too badly scuffed up.

"Okay, I'm looking at a word here; it looks to be in Latin or maybe Portuguese . . . I don't know what it means . . ." I droned on as I examined it. I tried sounding it out. "Mor-ee-quay? I think that's what it says, whatever that means. Is it a command or a binding?"

I was an educated man. I attended college across the street from this very property, and despite my trepidation about being there, I thought I was making sense. I'd continue in the same manner for the next few minutes, canvassing the entire area. Honestly, beyond those couple of details, there wasn't much to see. If Satanists were using this spot for their gatherings, I felt a little bad that they couldn't find better digs. But who was I to judge? I was certainly no authority on anything I was doing that night.

Shortly after the language lesson, I finished up and headed back to the main building to rendezvous with the others. Everyone had completed their tasks, and we executed a few more as a group.

The exploits of that evening would become the first-ever episode of our show, premiering on Staten Island cable access a month or so later. The shaky-cam footage, homemade music, and raw honesty made us a local hit. The most common comment we got during the run of that first season was, "You guys are crazy! I'd never go into the places you guys do!" That was our niche: the exploration of places others feared to tread. The history and information took a back seat to the outrageousness of the places and the things we did. Such was the luxury of youth. I could run around an abandoned site with my friends and not think about far-reaching consequences. As the years tempered the sometimes ill-choices a young man makes, I found myself with a different focus, and these days that focus is on education. My collective knowledge began back in my days kicking around that old gypsum plant, but a paramount lesson came from the editing room while we put together that first episode.

"Hey, Bri, come here; you have to see this!" Chris said with a smile. He was laughing as he called me over. Sitting down next to him in the edit bay, I saw he had my basketball court footage pulled up on the monitor.

He hit play, and the scene began. There I was, in a cadet blue outfit. A military-style button-down shirt with pockets all about it and a matching pair of cargo pants. The Airborne jump boots I wore kept edging into the shot as I pointed the camera down at the ground. A black belt outfitted with pouches and utility items made the look official. In my head, it was an approximation of the uniform seen in *Ghostbusters II*. It was the armor I wore to make myself feel protected out there. I felt like a kid again, wearing a *Ghostbusters* outfit, standing in front of the school as my mom picked me up in the family car with the homemade "No Ghosts" logo I'd taped onto the side.

I nervously watched the replay of my exterior adventure. It's one thing to live out something; it's another to see it played back on tape. Chris raised his hand and gestured to the screen. "Here it comes," he said.

What was I about to see? Had I captured something on camera? My anxiousness grew, as did the smile on his face. I was confused.

"Okay, I'm looking at a word here; it looks to be in Latin or maybe Portuguese . . ." I heard myself say again. The shot had the word framed dead center. The word in script had a capital letter and then lower-case letters strung out behind it. I was waiting for a ghost to jump out when Chris started laughing hysterically. "Mor-ee-quay? I think that's what it says . . ." echoed my voice from the past.

"Dude, look again—it says, 'Monique.' It's just somebody's tag on the ground!" he explained between guffaws.

I looked again. He was right. It was plain as day—it was neither Latin nor Portuguese, but English. In my defense, a lower case "n" in script does resemble a lower case "r" a little bit, especially when written hastily in chalk on the ground! All I could do in that moment was join my friend and laugh at my own expense.

Out there in those woods, I was so frightened that I allowed the fear to alter my perception, thus changing my reality. Looking back on that whole scene, it wasn't the site of a Satanic ritual at all. It was an old basketball court where some locals had had a few drinks and lit a couple of fires. Even in its ruined condition, the worn asphalt was the perfect canvas for a couple of impromptu tags and scribble. Looking again at the pentagrams, they indeed were stars within circles, but they were clumsily drawn, as if by someone who didn't know what they signified. Monique and her friends probably thought they'd scare whoever stumbled upon the symbols in the future. Monique, if you're out there, know that it worked. You got me.

This was yet another important lesson in perception for me. In the search for truth, what we see isn't always what is. Remember that Star Wars quote? "Your eyes can deceive you, don't trust them," Obi-Wan Kenobi said to Luke Skywalker. True, he was teaching him to use the Force in a fantasy sci-fi movie, but the quote always stood out as a wise one to me. Our senses and emotions are powerful tools we use to experience the world around us, but they are colored by our experiences and perceptions, meaning they are fallible. It's important to consider alternate explanations and re-examine the situation before coming to a conclusion. I had forgotten this basic tenet that night at the Augustinian Monastery.

After my embarrassment faded, Chris and I discussed how to work the scene into the episode. Creative editing? Cut it entirely? In the end, we kept the entire scene unedited. I felt it was important to show how my perception caused my state of mind in the moment. It is from our failures or weaknesses that we learn and grow stronger and conquer fear. Does this mean that I never get scared? Hardly— I get scared quite often. I just have learned to handle it logically. I apologize to the kid from MTV's Fear who was too afraid to go into The Hole. I now understand your trepidation in facing the unknown alone. But still, you had prize money on the line at the end of your effort. I just had a lot of laundry to do.

16

Two Steps Back

Fear comes in many forms. Even when you think you've conquered it, the emotion makes its unwelcome return. Hardwired into all of us, fear is a defense mechanism that never truly goes away, a throwback to days when we lived in caves with predators stalking us. In modern times, fear is often considered childish and irrational. The monster under the bed or in the closet isn't real. "You're just imaging things!" weary parents tell their children. Motivational speakers do their best to convince timid adults that fear is nothing more than False Evidence Appearing Real. But be they literal or figurative, monsters are sometimes real. Then again, they can be just figments of our own creation. As a paranormal investigator, I've learned a lot about this distinction over the years, but perhaps never so poignantly as a night I spent alone in southern Ohio.

I was on my way to the Cincinnati area after attending an event in Kentucky the previous weekend. My next destination was Bobby Mackey's Music World, where I would be holding my own event that Saturday. In between, I thought it would be nice to visit local friends and do a little exploring. I'd made it a point around this stage in my career to better experience the areas I visited, having missed out on a lot in previous years, only ever seeing airports, hotels, and convention centers. Every town had begun to feel the same, so I'd intentionally built time into my schedule to look around at each destination, connect with local culture and lore.

That week was fun. I visited friends, ate good food, and laughed a lot. My intellectual curiosity was piqued as I visited Noah's Ark

(The Ark Encounter) in Kentucky. I tried in vain to locate myself in the crowd concert scene of the new *Ghostbusters* movie. I ate a lot of Skyline Chili, and I drove many back roads as I explored the region. Because this Kentucky stop was part of a national tour, I also did my mandatory social media check-ins and live streams and even appeared on the ABC KY7 morning show. Friends and followers online gave me support through likes and positive comments. I also received many warnings and prayers in advance. Since I was going to Bobby Mackey's, plenty of "Bagans-ites" were convinced I'd get possessed upon entering the place. I was fairly confident I'd be okay, feeling almost fearless—until I returned to the Sedamsville Rectory.

Located a stone's throw from Wilder, KY, the rectory was a place I'd investigated on *Haunted Collector*. A place where I'd had an intensely personal experience. As Chris Zaffis and I investigated the basement (where else?), I got scratched across the back. The dreaded three scratches that all TV-educated investigators know is a sign of the demonic! Hardly so in that instance. As it turned out, on that case, we were dealing with an animal spirit. Shocking at the time, but it made sense. We later discovered there had been a dogfighting ring down there, and many animals had been abused in connection with it. The crew were all animal lovers, and such a thought was abhorrent to us. While I love all animals, I'm specifically a cat person. Yeah, dogs are great, but my choice and personality line up more with my feline friends. Given that fact, it is my fate that every dog desires to run up and jump on me—perhaps sensing my discomfort. John, Aimee, and Chris all had dogs and were unfazed by such behavior. And so it was in that basement. The canine spirit chose me to reach out to. Sure, I was physically affected by it, but I wasn't worried that my soul was in any danger.

Later on that same season, *Ghost Adventures* followed in our footsteps and toured the rectory with their usual demonic candor. They portrayed the place as a hotbed of evil. Whether it was or wasn't, I can't say—I wasn't there with them. But for me, it had been a very different experience. I was more concerned about the rough neighborhood and the abandoned church next door. I recall the production company hiring extra security to keep watch over the vehicles and equipment as we filmed. I've often quipped that I was more fearful of the living than the dead at this location.

Since that time, I'd heard news from those who had investigated the place or attended events there, and they all seemed to fall in line with those darker reports. Could I have missed something? Or was it that my energy didn't attract, perhaps even repelled, the things that others were claiming to have seen? Either way, when I knew I'd be spending time in the area, I reached out to see if I could pay the rectory a visit. No event, no fanfare, just a private walkthrough to see the place again with fresh eyes and a fresh perspective.

The caretakers had been experiencing much on the dark end, so much so that they didn't want to be there unless necessary. Knowing that, I thought they would deny my request, but they gave me permission—even better, they said I could stay the night if I wanted. The caveat being that they would not be there during my visit. It was an odd situation, but one I could not pass up. So, the Tuesday before my Mackey's event, I moved into the Sedamsville Rectory for the night.

As the sun hung low in the summer sky, I emptied my bags from the car into the lobby. I hurried so as not to allow the neighborhood eyes to see how much stuff I carried with me. The only eyes keeping watch belonged to a cadre of feral cats gathered in the driveway. They didn't allow me to approach them, but in my mind, they were there to welcome me, protect me, even. Those silent sentinels stayed until I finished unloading and then disappeared into the underbrush.

So, there I was, back in the rectory. Alone and in charge. At least that's what I told myself—I was in charge. But in charge of what? The building? My feelings? My creeping fear? Yes, I definitely felt odd. Taking inventory of the bags I had collected on the kitchen table, I grabbed a Dr. Pepper and took a big gulp. I noticed a few

familiar faces staring back on the wall opposite me—a photo of the *Haunted Collector* cast with the caretakers. I remembered posing for it some years back, which now felt like a lifetime ago. Be not afraid . . . they seemed to be saying. Or, in John's cadence: 'There's nothing to worry about, Hippy.'

With that momentary shot of confidence, I set out to do my initial walkthrough of the building. Now, let me be clear, I was not there to conduct an investigation. I would not be doing any EVP sessions, experiments, poking, prodding, or provoking of any kind—I just wanted to BE there. I wanted to immerse myself in the experience of simply existing in a haunted location. Given my history with the place, I also had something to prove to myself. It's easy to be brave when you have your friends with you. It's even easier to do so with a pair of cameras filming you. It's a different story when you're all alone. I felt like I was back in those woods atop Grymes Hill, searching for an abandoned basketball court.

I wanted to be sure I was totally alone in the place, so I went from room to room, opening each door and checking inside each closet, each cupboard, and inside every armoire and drawer. I made sure every window was locked and secure. I made sure all the outer doors were shut tight. Up in the attic, I found a ladder leading up to a hatch. It took me onto the roof, where I spent long moments watching the sun go down. The valley looked so peaceful. It was warm and quiet as a gentle breeze brushed the hair out of my face. Everywhere the light touched seemed blessed. Inside dozens of houses, families gathered for dinner. Cars driving on the highway were bound for their next adventure. In the distance, Cincinnati was gearing up for a night of possibilities. And me? I was on the cusp of another experience. I took out my phone and awkwardly snapped a few selfies, trying to get the best light, but no matter which direction I faced, I found myself squinting. Hashtag, forced?

As dusk settled upon the neighborhood, I ventured back down into the rectory to complete my sweep. From attic to first floor, I took an extra bit of precaution. I had sage with me and smudged each room and hallway I passed through to further ensure a peaceful night. Perhaps it was my imagination, but I felt, as the light from outside was dimming, that the warmth ebbed away. Not in the practical sense, as in temperature, but in a spiritual sense. I felt a nagging feeling tugging at me to hurry up and finish my sweep.

At one point, I found myself at the door to the basement. Okay, I have to admit—I was a little scared. Though I knew my last encounter down there was not malevolent, I still had reservations about being there during the night, as if other things would awaken during those dark hours. So, I never ventured below. I just smudged the door and commanded whatever was down there to remain down there and leave me in peace. In hindsight, I guess I was more than a little scared. That was my first error in judgment.

As I rounded a corner towards the back of the building, I came across a narrow staircase I had previously missed. I ascended it to find a small grouping of rooms. The last bit of light from outside was coming through the windows, giving the area a pale blue glow. I was able to see a tiny, unfinished bathroom, a closet with cleaning supplies, and a door that had a DO NOT OPEN sign on it. Despite the instruction, I knew I had to check it to be sure I was completely alone. That's when I heard shuffling come from behind the door.

Something thumped onto the floor. What was it? I took a moment to collect myself before turning the doorknob. The door creaked open to reveal an unexpected resident. A black and white cat sat neatly on his haunches in the middle of the room, staring at me with beautiful, golden eyes.

"Meow!" he said cheerfully, happy to have some company.

"MEOW!" I replied, happy to meet this new friend. He ran over to greet me, rubbing himself on my leg. "Hi, fuzzy! What are you doing here?" I asked, petting the purring animal. Looking around, I saw he had a food dish, a bowl of water, and a couple of toys. Someone was apparently taking care of him. I shot a quick text to the caretaker inquiring about the cat. She told me the transport coming to take him to his foster home would arrive on Monday. He was a guest of the rectory until then.

As you know by now, I love cats. I would have gratefully spent more time visiting with this one, but I had my sweep to finish. I petted his head again and continued my smudging. I was glad to have discovered him, though, since I now knew any noise coming from that part of the building could be his.

Shortly after, I finished my walkthrough and settled into one of the sitting rooms on the first floor. I would make that my living room until it was time to turn in. Walking around, I felt many eyes on me but was unsure if it was my imagination or spirits of the departed.

Hopefully, my efforts with the sage combined with my statement of intent would keep me from recreating a scene from *Ghost Adventures*.

The room was decorative yet sparse. Again, this was a rectory, not a hotel, so there were no amenities for the traveler, just basics for the clergy who would make this their home while serving the church. The decor was quite neutral, as it was in most other rooms. The floors and doorframe were natural wood, the furniture bulky and traditional. Paintings on the wall depicted pastoral scenes. Heavy, brown, full-length curtains blocked all outside light. One disturbing feature was the doorknob. Or rather, the damage sustained to the door around the knob. The metal plate reinforcing the handle had its top half ripped away. Just above it were scratch marks and a breach in the door itself. It did not appear to be normal wear and tear. This was damage caused by an attack, as if someone or something was trying to force the door open. It was difficult to decipher when it had occurred, but the fact that they'd left it as is was a bit spooky. I prayed that nothing would try to force my door open when I retired upstairs to bed.

So, there I sat. No television. The windows locked and shuttered. I only had what I'd brought with me for entertainment. That is unless I wanted to dive into the Bible and brush up on my Old Testament. I was alone in the Sedamsville Rectory, so I did what many of us do to banish uncomfortable feelings—I took out my phone and launched Facebook. Since I was on tour, I figured I'd check in with everyone and do a live stream. It also happened to be a Tuesday night, so it was time for "Tuesday Night Bri," an hour-long broadcast of me babbling, telling stories, and answering questions. (In researching this chapter, I went back and watched that broadcast to remind myself of the details of the room. At 44:08, I mention that "I will eventually write a book of my experiences, but I'm not in a rush . . ." Indeed!)

Doing "Tuesday Night Bri" ate up some time and made me feel better. My friends and followers gave me the shot of bravery I needed to get through the night. They distracted me from thinking about the place and the reports—and the basement. But when I signed off, all I had was myself again. I ate a snack and walked around the first floor a little bit, checking on a couple of noises I'd heard. I perused my social media once more and tended to a few neglected business emails. My plan before arriving was just to *be* there. It wasn't an investigation, so I didn't need to do anything other than what I would normally do at night. Admittedly, the surroundings had me on edge, and I found it difficult to relax. I can't say if it was the place itself or everyone's constant reinforcement of how bad it was that scared me, but to run out the clock, I figured I'd just sleep my way through it.

I'd spent most of the evening in that sitting room and felt like I'd "dug in" enough to feel secure. The bedrooms upstairs were foreign, and I really didn't feel like going up there. So I curled up on the couch and closed my eyes. Sleep came quickly, but it was not restful. My body was tense, prepared to react at the slightest sign of activity.

Eventually, morning came. I had places to be, so I didn't dally. The sun once again peeked through slivers of the window that the curtains failed to hide. I opened the side door to check the weather. The air was crisp and cool. Golden eyes peered at me from the bushes. Everything felt fine. But something still nagged at me.

As I collected my things and repacked the car, I did a quick tour of the place once more. I passed the door to the basement. Nothing had emerged from the depths during the night to torment me. It had been quiet. Upstairs, I came across the cat room again. The cat! I had forgotten about him. He meowed and purred and rolled on the floor, inviting me to pet his belly. What a fool I'd been. A damn fool.

Had I learned nothing these past few years? Working in the paranormal, I knew that intent played a huge part—intent and perspective. My perspective had shifted, changing me from a skeptic to a skeptical believer. In doing so, I had experienced much, which allowed me to fuel those beliefs. It seems it also allowed me to dwell in fear.

I had spent the night at the rectory with the intent of just being. I wanted to prove to myself that I was okay with what happened last time I was there and that I could be alone in a haunted place and have no fear. Or at the very least manage it. I'd failed. Firstly, my inability to go back into the basement showed I was not okay. I should have gone down there. Even if just once. I mean, why else had I come if not to confront what happened to me in the very spot it happened? Secondly, I'd done nothing but stay in that one room the whole time. I let the comments of everyone online sway my perspective towards fear. I was afraid, but I did nothing to try and conquer it. I avoided it. What's worse, I missed something that would have made it better, which was right in front of my face.

Instead of remembering the cat and going up to spend time with a furry friend, I allowed fear to incarcerate me. I let the thoughts of demons and malevolent spirits overtake my evening. I chose it, maybe unconsciously, but I chose it all the same. That was my own doing. I sank to the floor, and the cat came to sit in my lap. I crossed my legs and leaned back against the wall. As the room grew brighter with the rising sun, I sat there and listened to him purr. It was very comforting, yet I didn't allow myself the comfort. I just felt regret.

Soon, I would be leaving, and I'd never see him again. He looked up at me with brilliant eyes, full of life. Calm eyes, content eyes. He was happy there, happy to just be in this moment. My night could have been very different if only I'd changed my perspective and been more positive. This chapter would then have been about my cool night hanging out with a cat, not shivering alone in a sitting room.

Eventually, I had to get up and get moving. I petted the cat one last time and told him I was sorry for not spending more time together. I wished him well on his journey to his forever home. As I pulled the car out of the driveway, I paused to look back. I couldn't see the cat, but I knew he was in there. I couldn't see the feral cats in the yard, but I knew they were near. I mentally thanked them and said goodbye one last time.

The road called, and Bobby Mackey's awaited. With these lessons fresh in my mind, I resolved to take heed. No matter how much we think we know, there is always more to learn. No matter how advanced we think we are, there is always room for simplicity. Also, it's prudent to be in the moment, not allowing the past to define your future. Having learned that, I can say my night at the Sedamsville Rectory was not a waste. That weekend, I approached my event with positivity as well as an open mind. No devils showed up to darken my time there.

It's been a few years since my return to the rectory. I've never forgotten that cat and what I learned there. I wonder, if I were to come across him again, would he remember me? I wonder . . .

17
Keeping It Basic

L ooking back on my life, I can safely say I've had plenty of adventures. From the Dungeons & Dragons-inspired explorations of my youth to the supernatural sojourns in recent years, I've been blessed with interesting experiences. Some of my own making; others thrust upon me in the moment. One thing I will say, though, is that I often have trouble choosing a path. Which road to go down, what choice to make—even seemingly simple decisions can sometimes baffle me into inaction. And it's always been that way. Part of it, I believe, is my predilection towards examining all angles. Before making a choice, I prefer to examine and educate myself on the options. Even writing this book you now hold was an exercise fraught with stressful considerations—topic, flow, audience, style. I built one creative roadblock after another. In that respect, I was my own worst enemy, which is funny given that my goal was to become a writer in college.

I majored in English and minored in psychology. The former to develop my craft; the latter to better understand people and write believable characters. But until now, many years later, writing a book just hadn't come to pass. After college, I shot and edited documentaries, designing the graphics and artwork for those projects and others. I appeared on TV, on stage, in movies, and on more podcasts than I could count. I recorded several audiobooks and designed a card game with five unique expansions. I traveled the world, investigating and lecturing on almost every continent. I wrote forewords and afterwords (and even a few back cover blurbs) for books by my friends and colleagues. Simply stated, I'd found my way into almost every form of media I could think of, but I hadn't written a book. And in my mind, all my other accomplishments amounted to nothing without that one.

As my paranormal career progressed, people would always ask, "When are you going to write a book?"

"I don't know," I'd say with a shrug, then offer them a DVD or game in consolation. "I'm sure I have one in me—several, I think— but the time has to be right."

I'd try to sound as Zen as possible as if the Universe would use me as an instrument to pen the story of this incarnation. In reality, I was suffering the worst case of writer's block imaginable, though to call it that implies I'd actually begun writing and somehow gotten stuck. Not the case. Sure, I'd written things in conjunction with my other endeavors, but DVD jackets and rule books simply would not cut it. In recent years, my love of alliteration was compacted into 140 characters or less, further limiting my scope. But when I thought about a book (constantly), I just wasn't sure what to write and often felt crippled by my indecision.

As the course of my life developed, it became apparent that my first book would be about the paranormal, but what aspect or area? A collection of cases I'd worked on? A tome of process, instruction, and theory? I juggled these topics in my mind as years passed, but the right one never seemed clear. Sometimes I'd get as far as a document of ideas to be sorted out later, but it never coalesced into anything tangible. Nevertheless, time was on my side; I'd counsel myself. The longer I waited to publish a book, the more wisdom and experience I'd have to put in it. But waiting, as you know, is often very difficult.

As my shelf struggled to hold all the books I'd bring home from trips; I continued to ponder my own entry into this collection. Meanwhile, bookstores were beginning to close around the country, and I'd made every excuse in the book for not writing one. Despair set in, and I wondered if I'd ever write more than Facebook updates. My #Pfriday posts of philosophical questions for weekend reflection were hardly classic literature!

Desperate to choose a book topic, I echoed the sentiments of Dan Aykroyd's character in *Evolution*: "Let's take this ugly bag of snakes and lay 'em out straight!" Incidentally, I'd met him years earlier and credited him with inspiring me to walk this path of paranormal investigating. I even gave him a few *SCARED!* DVDs in the hopes of impressing him. He took a moment to evaluate the cover art before telling me I'd do well at conventions. He wasn't wrong, since we'd already begun making a splash at those we attended. Perhaps if he'd told me to write a book, I would have listened, although my indecision over a topic would still have been an issue. One might even say it haunted me.

Which reminds me of one of our early adventures on *Scared on Staten Island.*

***

It was early 2003, and we were traipsing about the ruins of the old Staten Island Hospital. What made this place so interesting was its division into two distinct parts. The first was the original building, a gothic-style mansion that resembled a castle. The second was a modern hi-rise, built decades later. Both were abandoned and in heavy disrepair. Of course, to a group of urban explorers, this was Disneyland. I'd grown up nearby and had always wondered what secrets lay inside the walls.

We'd scouted and explored all the buildings on the lot, but weeks later, when the time came to do the actual shoot, we came across something we'd missed. In the 1980s, an attempt had been made to turn the hi-rise portion of the hospital into apartments. Renovations had begun, and tenants had moved in. The top floor was turned into a penthouse. The other floors were converted into smaller dwellings.

Greg, Chris, and I found ourselves creeping through the first floor, waving our flashlights around, trying to act brave for the camera. Over the years, all the floors had suffered damage from the elements; many of the windows were broken, allowing rain and other nasty weather to take lease. It was apparent that the renovations to the building were never finished, as many areas were still under construction. Furthermore, looting of the valuable copper pipes and other parts had turned many of the walls into gaping wounds that never healed. Mold grew along the old carpets and walls like the bed of a rainforest. Fetid pools dotted the rooms as the sound of dripping water added to the sense of decay. Just another typical day for the SOSI Crew.

Every room we explored had a story to tell. As the local reports went, a company had bought the building and started converting it into living quarters. But halfway through, their money ran out, and the project was abandoned. Families that had already moved in were evicted—many suddenly and forcibly. The place was a ruin but still seemed as if some of those people had just left the day before. Pots and pans sat on stovetops. Worn pillows were arranged on musty couches. Toys and other relics of a life lived were strewn about the floor along with the debris.

I'll never forget a particular room on one of the upper floors. It was filled wall to wall with vinyl records. From Bach to The Rolling Stones, the collection was massive—and in relatively good shape! I remember digging through piles, selecting records to take with me. But I was reminded of the Urban Explorer's motto: leave nothing but footprints, take nothing but photographs. I forlornly looked at my treasures and put them back where I found them.

Another odd detail we noticed was the abundance of headless pigeons on all the floors. Some were tangled amongst the Venetian blinds; others were found inside glassware. We never found the corresponding heads to those poor avian bodies, which made us wonder who or what was doing the beheading.

We did encounter some living pigeons, but all of them were rather irate. These were the original Angry Birds, for any time we'd come near, they would flap about and strafe us until we ran off. It was one of these attacks that forced us into a hallway leading to a T-junction. The hallway we just came from hooked around and led to the rest of the floor. Ahead of us was the trimmed remainder of a hallway, with an access door we found to be rusted shut. To the left was a short hall dead-ending with two doors facing each other. That hallway looked like every other one on this level, save for a couple of details. The door on the right side had a chain across it; like so many others, it had apparently been placed there by the original landlord to prevent evicted tenants from returning to their units. It was drab and dingy, stained by years of water damage. The door to the left, though, was much cleaner and had no chain across it. Furthermore, light was coming from beneath it, and a pair of clean Timberland boots neatly placed on a mat to the side. We froze in our tracks!

We'd been wandering around this place for hours, looking for ghosts, avoiding birds, and trying not to hurt ourselves. We had gotten quite used to the alert mode we were in—but this was different. There was someone behind that door. As we listened, we thought we heard music. Could someone still be living there?

"What should we do?" I asked.

Greg and Chris looked at each other and made confused gestures with their hands.

"Maybe we should say something?" Chris suggested.

"Or maybe we should go knock on the door," Greg countered.

"I don't know. If we go right up to the door, that puts us too close if they end up being hostile," I said. Once again, my D&D experience had me thinking in terms of combat.

The next few moments saw our trio considering the outcomes of all possible courses of action. I wanted to call out from our current position. Greg wanted to knock on the door. We were deadlocked in an indecisive tug of war while standing in that ruined hallway. Chris had gotten silent as we ping-ponged back and forth. Finally, he decided for us.

"HELLOOOOOOOOOO!" he called out, interrupting our bickering.

Greg and I looked at him in shock and then at each other as we heard the sound of whatever was on the other side of that door turn lower. My heart was racing, and I prepared myself to high tail it out of there.

The door then opened, and a head poked out. It belonged to a young man, seemingly no older than 25, with a pair of sunglasses adorning his crown. A quizzical look on his face met the hesitant look on ours. We stared at each other for a moment until he broke the silence.

"Hey," he said, with a slight accent. He sounded Hispanic, but the monosyllabic greeting wasn't enough for me to tell for sure. A short, almost buzzed head of hair topped a round, brown face.

"Yo!" Chris countered back.

There we were, three guys in urban exploration gear—boots, headlamps, work gloves, backpacks—all carrying filming equipment, staring down a guy wearing a t-shirt, sweatpants, and flip-flops. It was an awkward and unlikely meeting.

"What are you guys doing?" the man asked.

"We're filming a documentary," Chris answered.

The guy nodded his approval. "Cool. You wanna come in?"

What a weird exchange. We'd been filming in the ruins of a place, not expecting to find anyone, much less anyone residing there! And yet we'd found one who was open to entertaining company? It seemed absurd, and we had another decision to make. There was no time to discuss it, but I was wary. I felt accepting his invitation could be dangerous.

"Sure," Chris said.

Well, there it was. We were going through the doorway at the end of the hall. The man nodded once again and waved us in. Greg gave me a dumbfounded look, and Chris shrugged as he led the way.

Entering this guy's apartment was like stepping through a portal to another world. Unlike the rest of the units on this floor, which had us worried about the dangers of rot and asbestos, this place was bright and undamaged. A halogen lamp in the corner illuminated the living room. I took a quick survey of the room to assess the situation, as well as the man himself. Mac from *It's Always Sunny in Philadelphia* would later call it an "ocular pat-down."

In the center of the room was a low-profile couch. Opposite it was a stack of storage boxes, atop which sat a television, several game systems, and a stereo. A cluster of wires snaked out from behind them and conspicuously trailed out a nearby window, which itself was hidden behind more boxes and a thick curtain. In between the couch and the entertainment center sat a couple of crates with a plank of wood across it. On the surface lay remnants of his dinner, an ashtray, and various bits of smoking paraphernalia. Around the edges of the room were more boxes. It was unclear if they were serving as makeshift furniture or filled with the products they advertised on the side—Sony, Hitachi, and Panasonic were some of the names I saw. While I cursively cased his joint, Greg tended to the politeness.

"Hi, I'm Greg. This is Chris and Brian. What's your name?"

"Eddie . . . Basic," he replied. A quick thinker this guy was. Chris would later point out that he noticed a pack of "Basic" cigarettes on the table. This Keyser Söze, who invited us into his place, did not trust us with his real name. Not like we cared.

Over the next few minutes, we exchanged forced small talk until it became clear there was little to say. That is, little we wanted to get into, despite our curiosity. Topics like, what the hell are you doing living here and all queries related to that. Expert conversationalists, we were not, nor were we investigative journalists. On the outside, this all seemed innocent enough, but there was something else going on here. Something most likely criminal, and we felt it best to put some distance between ourselves and Mr. Basic.

So we bid him good evening and told him we'd be steering clear of this floor as to leave him in peace. Both Greg and I were relieved to get out of there. Personally, I would take the dangers of an abandoned building over the unknown ones of a suburban squatter any day. But it did raise the question in my mind: was he aware of the things going on in this building? Furthermore, did it affect him in any way? So many questions I wish we would have asked, but in the moment, we were concerned with our personal safety.

Pondering the past, I am also reminded of my propensity for indecision and how it is alive and well in me to this day. If Chris had not decided for us in that hall, how long would we have stood there?

It's akin to my deliberating for years over how my first book should be written. I'd been standing in a figurative hallway junction when a friend of mine said something that brought clarity to my mind. "You're making it more difficult than it has to be. People love hearing your stories; why don't you just put them all in a book?" she suggested. Of course! It was so simple; why hadn't I considered it before? My cousin, Lisa Ann, had written two books that way. She wrote like she spoke and had some things to say, so she just said them. All the "what ifs" and "maybe I shoulds" faded away. The next day, I sat at my computer and just bullet-pointed the first batch of stories that came to my head. You're holding the fruits of that realization now.

As for the old Staten Island Hospital—well, here's the postscript to that story. Cue the music for the Where Are They Now end cards. Our show became very popular on cable access and cemented us as "those crazy guys" who went to places few others dared. The specific episode shot at the old hospital did not feature footage of Eddie Basic, but it did shine a light on the conditions there. Soon after it aired, we read in the paper that someone there known as "The King Squatter" had been renting out rooms on various floors. Because of our exposé, he was evicted and charged; any of those he fraudulently rented to were also removed. We never found out if it was Eddie Basic.

The building itself was then shuttered and put under tighter security. We never stepped foot in it again. It stood abandoned for many more years until it was torn down in 2011. Five years later, the gothic castle building followed suit. The old Staten Island Hospital is now all but a memory.

That was one of the many adventures I've had in my short time on this planet. As with all of them, there was a lesson to be learned that I didn't always recognize until much later. That theme seems to be echoed in many of the chapters within this book. But the one I took away from this experience was that when presented with life's complexities, you can lose yourself in analyzing possible outcomes. In an attempt to control that which cannot be, one runs the risk of becoming stagnant due to the fear of making the wrong choice. Sometimes it is best to pick a direction and sort out the details en route. While the devil is in the details, sometimes it is wisest to just keep it basic.

18

Knights of Meucci

I'd been investigating the paranormal for several years before having what I would consider a direct communication—meaning the first time I was willing to accept that such things actually happened. It's entirely possible that I'd come across previous instances of direct communication and missed the experience. I know I can sometimes be quite oblivious, though my awareness of the issue helps little with its management.

Skepticism is a healthy thing. Given the choice between it and naiveté, I prefer to err on the side of hard-headedness. While I consider myself a believer these days, I prefer to use the term skeptical believer. That is, I know that paranormal phenomena exist; I'm just skeptical of the people who report them. Yes, I do believe in the existence of ghosts and demons. No, I don't (always) believe they are the cause for footsteps on the floor above your apartment. Perhaps you should ask your upstairs neighbor to consider investing in a nice area rug.

It's a funny thing, belief (at the core of the word is "lie"). To believe, you literally must lie to yourself. That sounds harsh, I know, but faith in something you cannot prove must come with a certain amount of self-deception. A suitable story or compromise must be established to quell the sirens and red flags in your brain, telling you that something is amiss.

When you're a child, it's easy to believe. You have no reason not to, so you believe in everything. Santa Claus, the Easter Bunny, the Tooth Fairy—Jesus! These characters exist, and the only proof required is an occasional present, bar of chocolate, or currency placed under your pillow. That, and some days off from school. As you get older, though, you lose faith in most (if not all) of those figures. Facts are presented or discovered accidentally, and a new truth is revealed. But we adults, with our sophisticated and enlightened brains, often cling to the intangible. Why is that? When we discovered it was our parents eating the cookies and milk left out for good ole' St. Nick, the period of adjustment was short. Would we still get presents next year? Good, then all was right with the universe. But our religious figures do not fade so easily. Wars have been fought over them. People have died and continue to die in the name of the celestial banner one flies.

In a less inflammatory but still related area, many adults retain their belief in the continuance of the immortal soul after the body's expiration. Simply put, people believe in ghosts. Where's the proof? Thus far, it's all been anecdotal with a sprinkling of questionable data. But belief is often a fuel unto itself—a perpetual mindset that shuns opposition and clings to shards of supportive claims, no matter how dubious or decipherable they might be. As John Mayer put it, "belief is a beautiful armor, but makes for the heaviest sword, like punching underwater you never can hit who you're trying for . . ." The song is casting a sidelong glance at religion, but I could quote the whole thing and apply it to the paranormal. "Oh, everyone believes; from emptiness to everything . . ."

At this point, the rigid-minded skeptics would have thrown this book onto the floor (had they ever deigned to pick it up in the first place) for my quoting a musician rather than a scientist or anyone else with a Ph.D. To them, I say, "Oh, everyone believes, and no one's going quietly . . ." Yep. Mayer again.

I often pose this question to audiences: "In polite society, what are the two subjects people avoid discussing?" The answer, of course, is politics and religion. They're hot-button topics. TRUMP! I just alienated half of you. THERE IS NO GOD! I just angered the other half. It used to be that in any public gathering, people would avoid talking about such things to not offend those around them. These days the opposite seems true. Everyone is loud and proud about their most fervent opinions, no matter who they offend. I blame social media, or rather, *antisocial* media. Armchair critics have been given license to spew their opinions and seem to delight in being as incendiary as possible. Discussion and debate have degraded into arguing and name-calling.

I generally ask that question as a lead-in to the paranormal being an unintended amalgam of the two touchy topics. At its center is belief, and as a result, it is prone to the same complication as the other two—dissension based primarily on emotion surrounding the specifics.

Why such a jaded appraisal of humanity? To this, there is no simple answer, though I blame it partly on being a Knight of Meucci. The title is self-given and unofficial, but it's a charge I have taken solemnly and with a degree of irony. Please allow me to elaborate. Ask anyone who invented the telephone, and most will reply with Alexander Graham Bell, if they know any name at all. The average person would have no reason to contest that answer or dig deeper, so the incorrect information continues to be disseminated. But, in reality, the origins of the modern telephone began with Meucci.

Antonio Meucci (1808-1889) was a prolific inventor and not-so-subtle genius. He was always tinkering and working to improve upon his designs. The genesis of his "teletroffono" was born out of the necessity for him to speak with his bedridden wife while working from his lab/workshop in their basement. The mother of invention, indeed! During his life, he was often plagued with financial difficulties, which arguably changed the course of his destiny. He was forced to drop out of the Florence Academy of Fine Arts, where he studied chemical and mechanical engineering, due to a lack of funds. Poor business decisions and fraudulent investors caused several of his companies to fail. Further misfortunes later in life resulted in the patent on his teletroffono (essentially the telephone) not being renewed. That lapse allowed others to take center stage in the annals of history. At the time of his death, he was an impoverished and disgruntled man. These are the facts as recorded by several sources. Further information was gleaned directly from Meucci himself—postmortem, as it turned out.

We were investigating the Garibaldi-Meucci Museum in Staten Island, NY, when I first learned what I now repeat at almost every paranormal gathering and during almost every filming of *Paranormal Caught On Camera*: spirits just want their stories told. They want to be acknowledged. For those who have been wronged or forgotten, they want to set the record straight. It makes sense. We are social beings. In life, we gather and create communities. We foster friendships and start families. Our very existence is about the connections we make, which is why we seek to maintain those connections after death. Immortality can come from many different sources, be it the soul, a song, or just the utterance of one's name. So much of what we do in our lives is in service of the basic statement: I was here.

Now, this museum, the former home of Meucci, where he lived and died with his wife, was the subject of our latest documentary. Responding to reports of activity in the building and looking into the Masonic history of the site, we were excited to see what secrets awaited us.

We'd done our due diligence concerning the case itself. We'd pored through the history books and spoken to the museum curator as well as other volunteers who had witnessed strange occurrences there. We'd discovered that the house had been physically moved to this location many years earlier and that the basement was not originally part of the house. Giuseppe Garibaldi, Italian general and nationalist, stayed with Meucci during his years in exile. Some of his possessions were on display, as well as many of Meucci's inventions. The potential for residual energy at this location seemed high.

For the documentary, we conducted a two-night investigation. The first night, we approached it by the book: baseline sweep, stationary cameras aimed at the hot spots, trigger objects, and Singapore Theory experiments (also known as the Theory of Familiarization, which in the paranormal means the practice of recreating environments or stimuli that match the era of the personalities attempting to be contacted, to increase the chances of an interaction). I even invited members of Staten Island Paranormal, a group of female investigators who, ironically, all lived in New Jersey. Having investigated the museum previously, they'd already had experiences of their own.

The house was not large, making it easy to canvas the two floors and basement with detection equipment. Because of its small size, though, any inactive investigators were required to wait outside in one of the cars to reduce noise contamination. The neighborhood was fairly quiet, so we wouldn't have to contend with more than the occasional passing car. Additionally, if anything happened inside, backup would be mere seconds away.

The first night was marred with all sorts of technical difficulties. Lights turning off, cameras not working; these and other minor annoyances persisted all night. Aside from them, which one might be tempted to say were evidence of paranormal activity, there was little to note. We left with a couple of minor readings and the attitude that such things were typical. We were looking for evidence of the paranormal, and if it truly were as easy to find as many liked to think, it would not be a topic open to so much debate. The lukewarm results we obtained did not discourage us, though.

The second night was much different. It was as if a switch had been flipped ON. Perhaps the energy in the house needed to acclimate to our being there. Or maybe our energies were of the correct vibration that night to unlock certain experiences. Our first night there was December 2, 2006. The second was January 13, 2007. Would the research into the positions of the planets back then shine some light on why we experienced more? Perhaps it was just coincidence (a thought that will irk many who believe there are no such things).

Of the activity we recorded that second night, much of it was centered around the death mask of Mr. Meucci. The mask was on

prominent display in a cabinet that contained some artifacts of his career. Among them was a framed stock certificate from his communications company, a replica of his original telephone model, and a photo of Meucci himself.

I had measured aberrant readings from the mask throughout the night. At first, I thought they might be coming from the lighting fixtures within the display or the electrical box some five feet to the right. Those I was able to locate and identify, but the mask still seemed to be putting out some kind of signal.

As was our practice in those days, we each conducted individual sweeps of the location and then gathered together for a final group sweep. Chris and I had gone through the house with meters and other gadgets. Paul did a walkthrough to see if he could gain any information via psychometry (the supposed ability to discover facts about an event or person by touching inanimate objects associated with them). Lastly, Lisa Ann passed through to see what impressions she could get. Now, we found ourselves all gathered in the Main Gallery as the death mask of Antonio Meucci looked on.

At first, our attention had been distracted by a carved, wooden piano that Mr. Meucci had made himself. I was receiving readings from it, and Lisa Ann felt something might be hidden inside of it. Something inside the piano? What could it be? My mind raced with the possibilities. Earlier in the evening, I had been sent up into the attic crawlspace to track down something possibly hidden up there, as per Lisa Ann's feelings. All I kept thinking was that if there had been Masonic meetings and practices done here, perhaps some grand secret was also hidden here. Maybe this piano was not just a mere musical instrument. As we poked and pulled on it to try and find a secret compartment, she made contact with an unseen onlooker.

"Don't do that; I don't like that." Lisa Ann said. Her gaze was on the floor as if she were concentrating on something far away. She explained that she was getting impressions from a personality watching us. We were not alone in the room. Someone was standing behind her, she said.

We continued our search for a way to unlock the piano via a combination of keys played. Wobbly notes rang out, evidence of years of neglect.

Lisa Ann shook her head. "I still feel like somebody is behind me, and I just feel like he's laughing, like you will never figure it out. He's too smart," she announced.

We had the attention of whatever entity was with us. Be it out of concern or amusement; we were now the ones being investigated.

As if it did not want to be upstaged, the mask began to radiate energy again. My EMF detector whined its high-pitched drone, which intensified as I brought it closer to the display case. This no longer surprised me as it had been the central focus of the activity that evening. I asked the caretaker if she could remove the mask from the case and place it elsewhere in the room to see if the readings would subside.

She did so, and for a moment, it got quiet. But then the needle on my meter shot up again—the mask was active once more! But was it the mask itself or the unseen presence in the room?

"I'm feeling a cold chill on my back, Brian," Lisa Ann commented. I moved to where she was standing to scan her. Low readings showed that something was there, but I couldn't glean what it was. "Ooh, when you do that, I feel a warmth, as if you're blocking the cold that's been touching me," she continued.

It may have just been the excitement of the moment affecting me, but I could swear the area directly behind my cousin was noticeably colder. Moving to that space was like stepping outside into the winter air for a brief second. Using a non-contact laser thermometer, I confirmed that the temperature around her back was indeed dropping. The entire group looked around the room, hoping to catch a glimpse of who or what she was feeling. As investigators, we were at the heart of the activity but felt helpless to control the information coming in.

"I feel a male energy," she described, "he's laughing because he thinks this is all hysterical, quite frankly. He thinks he's very smart, and nobody would ever figure him out."

Once again, I walked over to the death mask, and the whine from my meter rose in volume. The room was small, and there were several of us in there, plus one if you counted the invisible occupant. It's not like he was playing hide and seek with us all over the house. But what did he want?

"Is that you, Mr. Meucci?" the caretaker asked. "Do you want to tell me something? I'm here every day."

"I swear I feel that person behind me again, and when you said that, I just heard, 'Yeah, I want to tell you I'm not over there, I'm over here,'" Lisa Ann reported.

"So why are you here?" the caretaker followed up.

Lisa Ann continued to look at the floor with her hands on her hips. She gave the appearance of one caught in many overlapping conversations and trying to keep them all straight in her head. I moved back to where she stood and ran my meter around her. It confirmed that something was there.

"He's following me," she explained. "He's right here, right on my left-hand side."

"Why are you following her?" the caretaker interjected, her tone icy.

It seemed as if a nerve had been touched. Understandable, given the situation, but the tension soon evaporated. A few in the group vocalized possible reasons why Lisa Ann was the point of contact. "It's because she's Italian," was the popular one.

"He says: because I take him seriously, and because I understand what it's like to feel like you have life's work to do and not just a job and that he wants to be taken seriously," Lisa Ann explained. She spoke as if the words were being whispered in her ear, and she was translating them on the fly. Once again, a nerve was hit.

"Who do you feel like doesn't take you seriously?" the caretaker asked. She had worked hard at her job and was very dedicated to it. The inference that perhaps this entity perceived her as being flippant about it caused instant distress.

The entire time, my meter had been going off, but while Lisa Ann passed on the words of her unseen companion, it decreased in volume, as if to let those words be heard more clearly. Was that even possible? Could the spirit control the concentration of its form to allow the meter to get quieter? Or was the effort required to deliver his message to our psychic a strain, diminishing the energy it had to maintain its presence there?

The caretaker's question still hung in the air, and it made for an awkward moment. A couple of us smiled at each other to break the renewed tension. Chris, our resident skeptic, shook his head. Suddenly, the meter's volume rose again, as if shouting at us—or perhaps identifying Chris as the culprit. That elicited a laugh in the group, and once again, the mood lightened.

"Does this make you think that we're not taking you seriously? Is this why you get upset when I let people come in?" the caretaker queried.

"Certain people, yes," Lisa Ann conveyed.

"Because I know you get upset, and I don't want you to be upset." The look on the caretaker's face was like that of a daughter seeking her father's approval. You could tell she was genuine in her words.

"It's very important to him that people understand the history and what he was trying to accomplish, and there's a lot more that people don't know about what he's done, and he says, in time, he will share that. But he's not a very trusting person," Lisa Ann said.

"With good reason." the caretaker put in.

"Some people come in here just for their own good, not to share his story. And that's what he wants; he wants people who will help him share his story." Now we were getting to the heart of it! No longer a moment of mystery, this had become a supernatural therapy session where walls were coming down, and truths were being told. This was someone unhappy with certain things he saw happening in this museum. He was angry and frustrated and, now that we were listening, he had a chance to vent his reasons.

"Is there anything we can do now, out of respect, to make our intentions clear?" I asked.

I wanted to do the right thing by this spirit. It is believed that spirits can hear our thoughts, so I wanted to be clear about who we were. A line from a Prince song that always stuck with me was, "If a man is constantly guilty for what goes on in his mind, then give me the electric chair for all my future crimes." There he goes again; you might be thinking. Does Brian ever think outside of movie and music quotes? While the source is from pop culture (Yes, it's from the *Batman* soundtrack), the philosophical notion behind it rings true to me. I'm a cynical New Yorker, so my thoughts often swing dark. Because of that, I always try to make sure my words and deeds broadcast otherwise. If this unseen world had access to all my innermost thoughts, then let me be judged by my actions. In this case, I needed to verbalize that we only had the best of intentions.

"He would like his picture on the show and would like a little introduction telling who he was," said Lisa Ann, who was in sync with the man, his responses pretty much instantaneous at this point. But who, exactly, were we speaking with?

"Is it Garibaldi, or is it Meucci?" Paul asked.

"Meucci," she answered, "because he's the bigger guy—it's definitely him." She turned and gestured to a large, mounted portrait of Antonio Meucci on an easel behind her. "He has that strong presence."

Skepticism aside, this was amazing to me. To conduct an investigation and get a few clipped EVPs and other random bits of evidence was what we had hoped for and were used to, but this was on another level. This place was called The Garibaldi-Meucci Museum, and here we were communicating with the man himself. This moment was not only an important one in my paranormal journey but also in shaping the man I am today.

Meucci was adamant about telling his story. Apparently, having a museum devoted to his life and achievements still wasn't enough. There was more to be done.

"He's beginning to fade . . ." Lisa Ann informed us.

Over the next few minutes, she communicated with him and got as much information as he was willing—or able—to provide. Some things were of a general nature, like his involvement with a secret society that made it difficult for him to come out publicly to challenge the theft of his inventions. Others were more specific and relevant to the present time. He claimed he knew one of the former workers at the museum was stealing. (She wasn't working in his best interest, so he did what he had to do to get rid of her.) That was of particular interest to me; the assertion that a personality from beyond the grave could influence the day-to-day actions of the living was unnerving. Think about it—our jobs can be difficult enough as we

struggle with deadlines, co-workers, and other such concerns. When was the last time you worried about the dead getting you fired?

One would hope that once you pass on, your responsibilities in this world would be over. According to Meucci, it comes down to choice. He chooses to return and check in on his former home. He's not there 24/7, but it is one of the places that still hold a particular interest for him. He cares about the house and the way it is managed. His story and its telling are also still very much on his mind. That night we were privy to his deepest concerns. In death, he still fears. He fears what history will say about him. He fears that the work he began in life will all be for nothing.

That, too, is a curious thing. The universal energy that bore the name Antonio Meucci for a time on Earth is still concerned about that identity's reputation. Might that seem small? Could it be interpreted as something that should be of no concern to one who has passed over into a greater plane? It's difficult to say, but that night I vowed to make sure many people knew his story. Chris did as well. In Antonio Meucci, we found a kindred spirit, one who worked hard but didn't get credit for it. A man whose toil and sacrifice offered little reward or accolades at the end of his day. It seemed unjust, and if we could help in fulfilling his wishes, we would.

On the road, during cases, and at times in our daily lives over the years, Chris and I would turn to each other and cry "Knights of Meucci!" as we acknowledged a situation wherein we felt as he may have during his days. We also would do so when we educated people about who he is and what he invented. Note I said is and not was. We learned that Antonio Meucci still exists and is involved in the crafting of his own story.

I suppose, in some way, I am a part of that story now—an extra, or character with one line, perhaps. Another connection was made that night at the museum, one that spanned the centuries. As I write this, I wonder if that connection is a reciprocal one. I often speak about the man and who he is. I've devoted a chapter in my book to telling how our connection came to be. I wear the adopted title with a sense of pride as it puts me on an ongoing quest. Does that now inform him of who I am and what I am about? On the Other Side, does Antonio Meucci speak my name? The adventure continues . . .

19

Let's Pfist Again

'm a gamer. I love board games, card games, video games, all types. When I was a boy, I spent many hours playing Dungeons & Dragons. It spoke to my creative nature—imagining and creating castles, encounters, entire worlds even. That opening scene in *Stranger Things* where the kids were playing in the basement? That was a perfect snapshot of my youth. And that time I went to the UpsideDown? Well, that's another story.

In the Eighties, the company that owned D&D was known as TSR, and they had begun a gaming convention out in Wisconsin called GenCon. I'd see flyers for the event at my local hobby shop and ads for it in my gaming magazines. My desire to attend grew. First, it was held in Lake Geneva before moving to Milwaukee. Each year, when my parents began talking about where to go on vacation, they'd bring up tropical locales and historical areas. Me? It was always Wisconsin. My dad wanted to be on the beach in the sun. My mom wanted to explore a quaint town somewhere. But I wanted to sit in a large gaming hall and play all day. Needless to say, I was always outvoted, but my dream of making it to GenCon never faded. Finally, as a young man in my twenties, I was able to lay eyes on its fabled halls.

Attending the convention was like being transported to another world, like being a kid again. I hadn't done much traveling at this point in my life, so the journey to a new city was exciting in itself. And once I'd arrived, being in the massive convention center was akin to being aboard a space station. I met and interacted with all sorts of characters and participated in interesting games. It was an industry event, so all the game companies were there running demos, giving out free swag, and putting on a show. I recall walking the aisles with my friends, Greg and Miska, filling up our plastic bags with whatever we were handed. It felt like Halloween! Each night we'd get back to the hotel and dig through our spoils. We'd spread out Promo cards, plastic game pieces, and postcard adverts all over the room. To this day, we laugh about tossing around the AOL Installation discs we somehow got saddled with. "How'd these get in here?" we'd scoff and then whip them across the room like frisbees! Those were good memories. Fun times.

As the years passed, I found myself at GenCon annually. First as an attendee, then as a volunteer for a game company. I was now one of the many people running game demos and handing out promo material, as were my friends and girlfriend at the time, who also volunteered for the same company. Swag from all the random booths was replaced by product from our booth, and at night we would return to the room and dig through it all. The company produced card games, so we would have dozens of packs to open. We'd call them pack-opening parties, as it was always exciting to rip open the packs, announce what good cards we'd pulled, and throw the wrappers on the floor. By the end of it, the room would be littered in a sea of foil with small piles of playing cards stacked on almost every flat surface.

GenCon had become a ritual for us, and the planning happened early in the year. My task was to book the rooms, the travel, the registration, and prepare us all for the adventure. When I was a boy, the event was still in its early years and finding its footing, and it would have been something to have seen it then. By the time I started attending, and even more so in my years volunteering, GenCon was huge. Over thirty thousand people all playing games in the same convention center was quite the experience! Borderline overwhelming.

Because so many people attended, hotel booking was a madhouse. Places sold out fast, and unless you wanted to stay outside the city and commute every morning, you needed to book quickly. Despite my tenacity, it all came down to server speed as the reservations were made online once the housing block became available. The convention eventually moved from Milwaukee to Indianapolis, partly due to the resources available, such as expo space and hotels. I had an easier time once this happened since I could never secure a cheap room in the housing block in Milwaukee. But I had to be there, so I booked more expensive digs. It seemed wasteful to secure a five-star hotel with grand amenities because we wouldn't be spending much time in the room. We'd be at the convention center from open to close, but prior to GenCon's move to Indy, a five-star hotel was the only lodging available. So I routinely booked our stay at the historic Pfister Hotel, a place I would later discover was haunted.

Built in 1893 and described as a "Grand Hotel of the West," the Pfister has hosted actors, musicians, and dignitaries. It was a beautiful and elegant hotel, and I felt very out of place. My ragtag group of gamers and I were fish out of water in the 307-room establishment that "combined contemporary luxury and the charm of the Old World," as described on its website. It was divided into two sections: the original building with its classic features and the new modern high-rise tower. When securing the reservations, I was always given my choice of section, and I always chose the old building. Something about it appealed to me. You could say it called to me. Walking through the grand lobby was like walking back in time, with its "extraordinary architecture and magnificent furnishings." Upstairs, the expansive hallways were reminiscent of those in *The Shining*. It had character. Even though it was a kick in the wallet every year, I felt it was worth it.

Returning to the room in the evenings was always a sight as we carried backpacks and bags filled with loot. We'd march with our heads held high past the uniformed bellhops and concierge desk as if we were returning from a battle. Their gazes examined us cursively, wondering who we were, their tongues a second away from inquiring, "How did you get in here?" The well-dressed, regal-looking other guests would give us a wide berth as they passed us in the lobby and hallways. By no means were we a rowdy bunch, but as Billy Joel once put it, perhaps we were laughing a bit too loud. Why shouldn't we be mirthful? It was an adventure that took us out of our regularly scheduled lives for an extended weekend once a year.

One particular year, a booking error resulted in us getting bumped up to a small suite. It was located in a corner of the hotel. Unlike the other rooms that could be accessed via a door directly off the hallway, we had a small corridor that led to ours. It offered a little bit of privacy and felt as if we were entering a secret area, adding to the allure of the place. The corridor was roughly seven or eight feet long—I remember we'd bunch up as we waited for whoever was in the lead to get their key out and let us in. You might be wondering why I devote any unit of memory to a hallway when there are so many other details. Do I remember the number on the door? The paintings inside the room? What view the window offered? Nope. Not a single one. But I remember this tiny walkway with unbelievable clarity. Let me tell you why.

Our crew had returned to the hotel in a rush one afternoon, eager to clean up and drop off our loot before the next panel or game or whatever was on our agenda. We had just enough time to stop at the room, then go back out for a quick bite before returning to the convention center. The elevator doors finally opened on our floor, and we piled out. We'd ridden up alone and passed no one in the hallway. Turning into our passageway, we queued up, anxious to get into the room. No sounds were heard in the hall beyond. It was the middle of the afternoon—just another quiet day at the Pfister. The door lock clicked open, and we all filed in. The door closed slowly behind us.

The whirlwind that was us getting ready for the next segment of the Con was like a pit stop at the Indy 500. The choreographed chaos took no more than two minutes. I was first in line to rush back out the door. And that's when I saw it. Splattered on the left wall, about two feet off the floor, was a goopy, brown substance. There was a thick mass at the center; the seeming impact created tendrils reaching out in all directions, in direct contrast to the orderly, lined pattern of the wallpaper. I'm being quite mundane in my description, but that was my reaction at the time. I stopped and stared for a moment, then backed up through the doorway and closed the door so I could open it again as if to reset the scene. Yep, still there.

"What's the holdup?" Miska asked. I could have just said what I thought, but I figured I'd let him see for himself. I stepped aside and let him pass. He, too, stopped in his tracks. He turned to me with a befuddled look on his face. Next up was Greg, who followed suit.

"It's really simple, guys," my girlfriend began, "one foot in front of the other, alternate and repeat." She was about to continue her taunt when we parted to let her see what we saw. Her mouth was agape, but no sound emitted for a long moment. Then, "Oh my god, somebody shit on the wall!"

It was an absurd statement, but the evidence seemed to fit the description. Obviously, it wasn't any of us. We may have been rushing to get ready in those two minutes, but I assumed we would have heard someone explosively relieving themselves in our alcove. It just didn't make any sense! As I mentioned, the floor seemed deserted when we got back. Who would have run all the way to our area, pulled down their pants, fired a fecal volley onto our wall, pulled their pants back up, and then escaped without a sound? I couldn't fathom such a thing happening at such a swanky place anyway, but the physical facts just did not line up. If it were another guest, they would just go to their room. If it were a maid or bellboy, the risk outweighed the statement being made, and besides, we'd been very good to the hotel staff. I saw no reason to draw any wrath from them. But there it was . . . in all its muddy glory. To further add to the oddity of the moment, the specimen had a stout consistency about it, as if it had been there for a while, giving it time to solidify. Also, there was no odor.

Gentle reader, I bet when you picked up this book, you had no inkling that you would be reading such a detailed description of poop. It's much like the feeling the four of us had when we realized we'd have to phone downstairs to get someone to clean it up. It was the absolute last item expected on the list of things we'd be doing that day.

Picking up the receiver, I described exactly what we had seen to the front desk and sheepishly asked for housekeeping to come up and tend to it. Man, would we have to tip them well at checkout! An annoyed staff member was up shortly to survey the wall. Like a CSI tech at a crime scene, he eyed the evidence and then us, trying to figure out if it was a disgusting prank and if he should take it out of our deposit. I related to him exactly how we discovered it. Reluctantly, he accepted our explanation. We stuck around to receive the worker who had drawn the short straw. He, too, had to endure our explanation. By this time, we were late for whatever we were rushing to get back to. I injected some displeasure into my tone as we left, citing that I didn't think such a thing would happen inside their impeccably reputed hotel. But there were stories about the hotel, ones I would not hear until years later.

***

Time passed. The world changed, as did I, and it had been several years since I had traveled to GenCon or Milwaukee. Ultimately though, I found myself on a plane headed there for work. The ad agency I worked for was pitching Miller beer, so I was sent out to tour the brewery and film some interviews. It was good to be traveling again, as I spent most of my time those days cooped up in an edit bay watching the world through footage on my monitor. As the cab picked us up at the airport, I asked the account rep who came with me where we were staying. She took a moment to fish through her bag and then produced a paper with our travel details.

"It's called the Pfister. Should be nice," she answered.

I immediately perked up. Of all the hotels in the city, what were the odds we'd be staying at that one? Well, the number is not astronomical. A Google search reveals around 22 hotels in the downtown Milwaukee area, so the answer would be one in twenty-two. But at the time, it seemed like quite the fortuitous coincidence. It was a beautiful hotel that I knew I would be comfortable in, and it showed that my company wasn't going to be cheap on our accommodations. Ironically enough, I'd forgotten all about the scat incident.

Standing in line in the hotel lobby, waiting to check-in, I looked around and felt as if the walls and paintings on the ceiling were welcoming me back. My co-worker was impressed with the decor. I mentioned I'd stayed there before, and that seemed to impress her further. I thought maybe we'd get to see the tower portion, but our reservation put us in the old building. That was just fine with me. Despite my nomadic nature, I do relish returning to familiar places as a jumping-off point for new adventures. As we received our keys, I wondered if I'd been placed into a previously assigned room. Taking the elevator up, I still had a mental block on the excremental event of the last visit. I'm not sure why; it's not like it was a traumatic event or something that scarred me for life.

"I heard this hotel is haunted," she commented. It was well known around the agency that I was into the paranormal. Most viewed it as a kitschy hobby that was right up there with boardwalk fortune-telling and astrology. The average worker at my company aspired to be like Don Draper, not Fox Mulder. Despite this, her comment was made in earnest. "Did you experience anything in the past when you stayed here?" she followed up.

"No, never saw anything here," I began. But as we exited the elevator and started down the hall, I stopped at the sight of a small passage to the left. The haze cleared, and I continued, "but this one time . . ." I paused again, thinking that this woman would not want to hear a tale of feces and its phantom owner.

There it was—the record just skipped.

I had forgotten about the fecal incident because we had never gotten to the bottom of who did it. As such, it had become just another story of travel misfortune, like flight delays and lost luggage. My headspace at the time had been in card games and dice, so the paranormal explanation hadn't even occurred to me. Even if it had, I would have thought a passing spirit would leave evidence along the lines of ectoplasm, not ghost guano! That afternoon, all those years ago, we'd been the victims of a spectral drive-by!

This was a grain of sand that took a long time to be shaken out of my clothes. Between the actual event and my understanding of it, over a decade had passed. There are plenty of reports detailing spirits leaving behind other kinds of evidence, but I was hard-pressed to find any reports that backed up my experience. I had a hard time finding proper Google search words to avoid the wrong kind of result. Ghost Poop, while amusing, was not exactly what I was looking for.

So now that I've accepted the possibility that the scat on the wall had been of paranormal origins, I am left to ponder why I (or we) were chosen for this particular message. Was this a spirit that had been trying to contact us in other ways and felt out of options? Was it a ghost that specifically haunted the hotel—was it the room, the floor, or the time (day/season/year) that allowed the manifestation? Were we the trigger, or would this have happened regardless of who was in the room at the time? I still don't have answers to any of these questions. Perhaps the phenomenon occurred so that I may one day ponder an origin beyond the merely physical. Thankfully, it's never happened to me again, so I've never needed to become an expert on spooky bowel movements.

My takeaway is this: you need not go looking for the paranormal. It is everywhere. While sometimes startling and confusing, it does not exist outside of what should be. Paranormal phenomena, at least for now, are beyond our ability to understand them completely, but that does not mean the Universe is broken. It's operating exactly as it should and in many ways beyond our comprehension.

After all these years of investigations and research, it is my assertion that you don't have to go to a so-called haunted place to experience the paranormal. I think there are locations where it may be easier to encounter such activity, but it can also occur where you are right now. Just as human beings are all over the planet, so are spirits. Everywhere is haunted. Where we are, they are, for we are them, and they are us. Perhaps we are their UpsideDown, not the other way around.

In some ways, I feel like playing Dungeons & Dragons as a kid prepared me for adulthood in the paranormal. Dreaming of other worlds filled with incredible creatures, going on adventures where I had abilities beyond the normal, and handling situations that forced me to consider all the possibilities—almost sounds like the paranormal. *Almost*. Many adventures still await me. Has my reaction time to the unknown improved? I guess we'll see.

20
It's All in Your Head

My head felt like it was caught in a vice. I was no stranger to headaches, even of the migraine variety, but this was something different. The pressure behind my eyes made it difficult to keep them open. Looking at even the dimmest light felt as if I were staring into the sun, leaving me blind and in agony. Time had slowed to a near stop, each second marked by the pounding in my head. The pain was all I could focus on.

Standing was nearly impossible as the room around me became a blur of dull colors. I sank to one knee and massaged my temples in an effort to clear my vision. I felt nauseated. To pass out into murky darkness would be an improvement, an escape, but doing so in the hallway was not what I wanted. I fought to compose myself.

"What have I done to wrong you, Andrew?" I asked.

The pounding in my head quickened. The vice tightened. My eyes hurt worse, open or closed. It seemed my question had fallen on deaf ears or unsympathetic ones.

I had already taken two doses of my go-to painkiller but found no relief. Sadly, it was no surprise to me. Thus far, every visit to the Lizzie Borden Bed & Breakfast came with an assault on my senses. As you may have suspected, I didn't honestly believe my headache's origin was supernatural. I spoke the name of the family patriarch in the way an atheist invokes God when praying at the porcelain altar after a night of drinking. It was a last-ditch effort, motivated by desperation and colored with insincerity.

I managed to stand back up and look around. I was on the second floor, in the back of the house, just outside Andrew's room. The pain didn't increase or decrease in conjunction with my position in the house; the torment was constant and had characterized my relationship with the Borden residence for several years at this point. Any time I set my course for Fall River, MA, the ache would begin and grow stronger until it hit maximum tolerance. There were times I planned to visit and woke up with it. Other times, I'd simply be in the region and decide to drop by, then feel the ache start as if confirming my new travel itinerary. It was uncanny, and I would joke about it to others while secretly being concerned.

"The house knows you're coming. It's getting ready for you . . ." a psychic once told me a week prior to my next visit. She wasn't specific about the source—was it the house itself or a personality inside the house? Psychics—always giving out information you didn't ask for, yet unable to give you the details you do want!

I shrugged and laughed it off as I always did. I knew I'd be in severe pain in a week, although I hoped that maybe this time would be different.

Looking back, I can't figure out why the house would take issue with me being in it. The owner Lee-ann was a friend of mine. I made it a point to stop by when I could, just to say hello. No ulterior motives, no edging for favors or de facto publicity; I just wanted to maintain that bridge. The friends I've made in the paranormal are important to me. As I search for the links to life beyond death, I very much appreciate the living connections I've made. Checking in on the empire is how I would describe it. Recalling the old saying, "The sun never sets on the British Empire," I was establishing a modest one of my own.

I'd been to the house several times as event support for others, either filming or assisting. Eventually, I went there with *SCARED!* to film a documentary which later led to a triad of events dubbed The Retrial of Lizzie Borden. In each instance, respect and deference to the wishes of the owners were taken, so I saw no cause for offense. And yet, my association with the house resulted in physical torture. Who or what was behind it?

Lizzie Borden took an axe,
gave her mother 40 whacks.
When she saw what she had done,

she gave her father 41.

Andrew Borden now is dead,
Lizzie hit him on the head.
Up in heaven he will sing,
On the gallows she will swing.

Time has passed in Fall River,
where mem'ry can't forgive her.
In'trest there will never wane,
Other heads will suffer pain.

Could it have been Lizzie attacking me? Or whoever was the actual murderer? Perhaps it was because I was male, or a skeptic, or a combination of several personality traits. Did I remind her of her father in some way? It seemed like a stretch to me.

The more likely explanation was that I was picking up on the echoes of the massive trauma delivered to the skulls of both Andrew and Abby Borden. It was an empathic vibration. But why did it affect me when I wasn't in the house and, furthermore, why did it start when I would decide to visit? I could understand it happening when I was inside the house, especially in the rooms where the victims were found. But hundreds of miles away? Were the headaches warnings? Or messages of some kind?

Standing in the hallway outside of Andrew's room, all I could think about was getting relief. Medicine never worked. Massages, pressure points, hydration, reiki, and even prayer—all of them were useless against the cephalgia. I had historically been lousy company when I was there due to the debilitating pain. Only when I found myself on I-95 heading home did it ever subside.

After asking Andrew if I had committed any transgression, the only answer I received was silence. Stepping into his room, I looked around. The house had been turned into a bed and breakfast in recent years but still styled as it had been in the late 1800s. It was quaint and comfortable, and if you did not know about the grisly double murder that took place there on the fateful afternoon of August 4, 1892, you would probably feel right at home.

I'd stayed there many nights, in several different rooms. Each one was homey and had a cheerful feeling when the sun shone in through the windows. Occasionally, you'd catch a glimpse of a black tail darting by as the resident black cat Max would aloofly inspect the guests. In the mornings, the smell of scrambled eggs and pancakes filled the air. It was quite an inviting place to stay—save for the migraine-level headaches.

In Andrew's room, I noticed some random collection of coins on top of a bureau. I could count no more than a dollar and a half scattered across the dark wood. Later, I mentioned that a guest must have forgotten to pick up their pocket change. It was explained to me that the coins had been left there as "Andrew's Bribe." Guests of the house would often leave money there for Andrew. He'd been a frugal businessman, so it stood to reason that the language he spoke, even in death, was a fiscal one. The motivations for bribing Andrew's spirit varied. Some people did so to ensure a quiet night, free from spectral visitations. On the opposite end of the spectrum, others placed their bribe as a fee to hopefully bring forth the patriarch during their visit. Honestly, the whole concept of making offerings to the unseen was a new one to me. I wondered if it ever worked. The guides in the house would relate the recent tradition to their tours with a smile. It added to the mystique of the house; that I could not argue.

Maybe I should leave some change myself next visit . . .

The next time I found myself at 92 Second Street, the thought crossed my mind again. I briefly greeted Lee-ann and my friends in the gift shop and then headed upstairs. It was a beautiful day that was already marred by the booming pulse of my head pounding. Reaching into my pocket, I fished around my keys to grab a handful of coins as I entered the rear master bedroom.

"Okay, Andrew, we're going to try this. I don't mean any disrespect . . ." I spoke softly to the walls. I'm not sure how much I had in my hand, but it could not have been much, even by nineteenth-century standards. I didn't want to offend by the amount, but I would try it all the same. I was going to bribe Andrew Borden to leave me alone.

"Here you go, sir," I said as I settled the change onto the bureau. I stood silently and listened to the afternoon for a few moments. Cars drove by from time to time. Somewhere in the neighborhood, a dog barked. Inside the house, all was peaceful. Dust particles danced in a beam of sunlight through the window. My head still pounded, though. What did I expect, magic?

I can't recall exactly when, but my headache did go away. It was either later that visit or the next; on that, I am fuzzy, but the important detail is that I was pain-free! From that time forward, I have never had headaches again at Lizzie's.

But why not? This forces me to examine the situation again. Be it the affectation of a specific spirit or the result of a burgeoning empathic ability; something was different. You can't bribe a feeling. If this was the doing of a personality, was it indeed Andrew? Considering an even darker possibility, perhaps another entity had taken up residence in the house, one attracted by the macabre interests of its visitors. The celebration of a heinous crime is a bit morbid. I know neither the owners nor the staff take it flippantly or make light of the event, but I can't speak for every visitor who has ever laid down in the spot where Abby was found or sat in the same position as Andrew in his picture from police evidence. The energies of people with this type of mindset do get left behind and collect, which could certainly call in other energies.

Let's continue down this path for a moment. Perhaps a spirit arrived and was fed by the attention of curious tourists. The voices calling out to Andrew, Abby, and Lizzie would be answered, but not by their actual namesakes. The more attention this entity received, the more it grew accustomed to its new identity. Eventually, it settled into a new role that became synonymous with the house itself. But if that's true, why did it affect me in the way that it did? As far as spirit attacks go, I've heard of much worse, and I'm thankful that this one—if indeed it was a spirit attack—never escalated.

Then there is the matter of the money. I left it for the spirit and with the request that I be left alone. Even though I'd envisioned Andrew Borden when I did it, perhaps the squatting spirit identifies with that name now. "Andrew" demanded to be acknowledged, and perhaps I hadn't done so in the manner in which it was accustomed.

In my research, I have come across mentions of spirits that associate themselves with the land and the home. Various cultures have different names for them, but all seem to fall under the general description of a fairy. They are a race of creatures that are generally unseen except by those with a clairvoyant gift. Unless they wish to be seen, that is. Like humans, they have free will and, as such, run the gamut of personalities. Some are benevolent and wish to help humans; others delight in causing mischief and bringing harm to them. If a household acknowledges and respects them, offerings can be left to curry favor with fairies. In return, fairies can help with day-to-day chores and bring general good fortune.

The lore also states that offerings left at lakes, tree groves, and other sacred sites can allow fairies to help ward off illnesses and misfortune. Could fairies be living on Second Street in Fall River? And if the people there anger the fairies, could things go horribly wrong? Like, say, a double murder.

Now, I'm not insinuating that a gang of fairies murdered Andrew and Abby Borden, but we have heard of cases where supernatural influences affected the living to do unspeakable things. Almost sounds demonic. Murder is an evil act, for sure. There are specific demons who deal in the commerce and evaluation of human lives— I dare not name them—who could also be responsible. I shudder to think of my friend having a demon (or demons) in her house and business.

It is possible that demons have been at work in that neighborhood for some time. Forty-four years before Lizzie allegedly swung her ax, there was another tragic double murder on Second Street. More accurately, a double murder and a suicide. Eliza Darling Borden, the second wife of Lizzie's great-uncle Lawdwick, drowned two of her three young children in the cellar cistern, then went upstairs and took her own life. This horrible occurrence took place next door to what would later become Andrew's house. So much death in such a concentrated area—four total murders and a suicide. Is this evidence of sinister machinations at work? Few speak of the former event because, while tragic, there was no mystery surrounding it. There was no trial, no media circus, no made-for-TV movies, just three grave markers, two chiseled with very short lifespans. Perhaps a debt had come due. Maybe it was madness. I do not presume to know why a demon chooses the methods and timing that it does.

Okay, we've gone down that path far enough. The last thing I want to do is put a rumor out there that the Lizzie Borden House is infested with demons! Let's return instead to my prior line of thought—fairies.

As I mentioned, there is the matter of the money. I suppose you could say that my pocket change was an offering. It could also be seen as a transaction. Either way, it seems to have worked. Even if I didn't see to whom or what I was offering payment, it was acknowledgment all the same. I spoke and was heard. It was also a one-time payment. As I've said, I've never again had headaches when visiting Lizzie's. So perhaps it wasn't the currency value, as I'd worried when I left it, but the effort that was important. Maybe it really was the thought that counted!

That's what makes the paranormal so difficult at times. There are so many variables to consider. The reasons for my headache number easily in the dozens. Even if I cannot identify them all, only a couple could be considered paranormal, and pinpointing one would open up a whole other subset of variables.

Examining the facts I have in front of me, I feel no closer to finding out the truth behind my headaches or the coins that seemed to end them—only more questions, which in turn have introduced me to concepts I'd had yet to consider. Even while writing this, I veered into research that I had not intended to do for this chapter.

I've been back to the Lizzie Borden Bed & Breakfast more times than I can count. It is a place where friends are. It is a place that taught me a few things and continues to teach me each time I go. Many ask me about it, fixated on the first square on the board—did Lizzie do it? My answer is always the same: How many times do you suppose people go in there and ask questions such as "Lizzie, why did you do it?" or "Andrew, are you mad that you're dead?" I'm an impatient New Yorker, so I get annoyed if I am asked the same question even twice. What a droll existence for these spirits if they actually are there. To have to answer the same questions over and over sounds like a certain kind of hell to me!

Imagine for a moment Lizzie or Andrew were there at the time the questions were asked or that the asking brought them forth. Having received the same query so many times over the years, what makes one think they would be inclined to answer truthfully, if at all? It's a hubris we often display—that our questions should compel answers on demand. I'd wager that if she is there, Lizzie must have developed a twisted sense of humor about these questions by now, sometimes having fun with the curious visitors. But I suspect it's been some time since she's been to her old home. The crime remains unsolved, and I think it always will. However, if my journeys in the paranormal have taught me anything, it's that whenever I think I know something definitively, I'm usually off the mark.

So, what did I encounter in the Borden house? A demon, a fairy, an empathic echo? Andrew, Abby, Lizzie? The jury is still out. Maybe it's all in my head.

***

Since the writing of this chapter, my dear friend Lee-ann Wilber has passed away. It happened shortly after the sale of the Lizzie Borden Bed & Breakfast to an outside investor, and I do believe it broke her heart. Mere days after she left us, her beloved cat, her familiar and earthly spirit animal, Max, also passed. His watch had ended, and now both of them travel realms I can only speculate about. I do hope we cross paths again someday.

21

Hope on Oak Island

The brisk autumn air blew strands of hair across my face as I scanned the excavation site. The sky was pure blue with fluffy white clouds trailing lazily across the landscape. Tall green trees reached upwards to meet them, creating a snapshot suitable for a postcard. *Wish you were here,* it would say, and if there were no other indications, it would seem a curious dichotomy of nature and chaos.

The mighty forest had been pushed back from this spot and replaced by massive digging equipment. A colossal shaft had been quarried and was dwarfed only by the gigantic crane parked next to it. No ordinary hole in the ground, this one was the focus of a treasure hunt that's been going on for over two hundred years. I was standing on Oak Island, next to the fabled Money Pit.

***

Two weeks earlier, I'd arrived home from work to find a message from a production company saying they wanted to talk to me about an opportunity. In the paranormal field, such contacts are common and don't often pan out, so my excitement level was low. I noted the producer's name and Los Angeles phone number. Due to the three-hour time difference, he'd still be in the office—I could give him a call and find out what he wanted that night!

I'm no television veteran, but I've spoken to enough producers and production companies to be cautiously optimistic when dealing with them. Associates of mine would practically leave their jobs and tell the wives they were hitting the road based on just one query email from a producer. Not me. Skeptical to begin with about the paranormal, I was especially so regarding those looking to exploit it for television. Besides, any such call I'd gotten in recent days was either to inquire about what my old *Haunted Collector* buddy was up to or pitch me a show where I'd be the tech guy for some random person I'd never heard of.

Don't get me wrong, it was nice to be considered. I felt a certain degree of pride in still being on the relevance radar, but several years had passed between the end of my old show and the present. I'd grown. I'd evolved. I was no longer content to play second fiddle to another figure. Cast me on another show with John Zaffis, and I'd follow him wherever he wanted to go, but few others have earned such status with me.

The call was brief but productive. Having gotten my name from another producer with whom I'd spoken before, he already knew who I was and what I was about. Our conversation had gone so well that I was to be emailed an Appearance and Materials Release later that evening. It was the show biz equivalent of a quickie Vegas wedding. The paperwork was received, signed, and returned. I would appear on *The Curse of Oak Island: Drilling Down* in two weeks!

While the show content was heavy on pop-archeology, it did have "curse" in the title—some attention eventually had to be paid to its possible paranormal nature. I had been tapped to perform a mini-investigation at some of the hotspots on the island. Could some of the things reported truly be supernatural in origin? A trip to Halifax, Nova Scotia, sounded like the kind of adventure I'd been waiting for. Because it wasn't a paranormal investigation show, I'd be expanding my visibility to the public, and the thought of going to an active dig site where relics attributed to the Knights Templar were possibly buried got me very excited! The words "Ark of the Covenant" had been mentioned to me more than once by the producers, as well as friends of mine who religiously watched the show. Perhaps I needed to purchase a whip and a fedora for my trip.

Two weeks went by in a flash. I suddenly found myself driving across that narrow land bridge leading to the island. The forest beyond stared back at me as if to inquire about my business there, all the while guarding any view of what lay within. Directly on the other side of the bridge was a cluster of buildings flanked by a dusty parking lot.

I pulled in and surveyed the scene. The sun shone brightly that day, enhancing the colors of everything the light touched. The waters glittered with promise. It was a beautiful vista to behold, yet something was amiss.

I heard no creatures. I saw no birds or squirrels or any sign of life save a couple of people taking pictures by the Interpretive Centre. Turning my gaze to the trees again, I gave them a good look. The island knew I was there, and it was holding its breath. It was sizing me up, waiting to see what manner of man I was.

A practice I began many years earlier, any time I would enter a purportedly haunted place, was to silently introduce myself and greet the spirits who may be listening. Feeling as if something older, more elemental, was evaluating me at that very moment, I felt it prudent to continue the tradition. *I mean no harm,* I thought. *I'm here to do a job, and I mean no disrespect. Grant me permission to walk these pathways and discover those who watch over them.* I usually stammered as I did this. The words were never pre-planned, nor were they ever the same. I just said what I felt in the moment since I assumed that the spirits would see my intent and detect any falsehood.

As I finished my silent introduction, a sliver of worry slipped into my thoughts. What if the island rejected me? What if I was unable to collect any evidence? I'd only be there a short time, and as I always maintain, spirits don't act on cue.

Having seen many episodes of *The Curse of Oak Island*, I was familiar with the activities going on there over the years. A hunt for a mysterious treasure that lay hundreds of feet below the ground, allegedly buried by pirates, or perhaps even the Knights Templar, had kept viewers glued to the exploits of the Lagina Brothers for five seasons already. Following in the footsteps of other treasure hunters, they mixed methods of traditional archeology with modern technology in their attempts to capture the prize. Several deaths have occurred in pursuit of this treasure, thereby spurring the legend of a curse protecting it. As it has been told, there will need to be seven deaths before the treasure can be unearthed. Six have already gone before. One remains. Who will it be? I sure as hell didn't want it to be me!

Such thoughts were my companions as I continued to look around the area. Two buildings, which served as War Rooms for the diggers, sat just to the right of the Interpretive Centre, a museum where visitors could view the artifacts uncovered thus far. A dirt road snaked up between them, leading to a gate arm blocking off the rest of the island from tourists. Beyond that, I could see a grouping of trailers where the production team would be based.

I was on time, but no other person was visible. No one was at the gate to greet me, only the sounds of the wind rustling the branches of the nearby trees. I still felt as if I were being watched, and the absence of crew gave me the impression that the island was definitely the one in charge. As if it asked for this time alone with me to decide if I was worthy.

I've always preferred to err on the side of humility, but this was a stare-down that required confidence. I'd put in the years, learning all I could, teaching what I knew, and helping others along the way. I'd paid my dues. I'm sure I was not the first person the production company contacted, but the fact that I was on the list meant something. I deserved this. I was worthy. Time to get to work.

Hours later, I was riding in a golf cart with Matty Blake, the show's host, as he was prepping the first shots of the day. The wilderness was now alive with human activity. Producers and techs swarmed all over like ants around an anthill. They were equally as industrious, each one with a specific task to complete. I watched the organized chaos and smiled. It took me back to days on the road with Ziggity, Badger, and the others.

We toured the entire island and conducted mini-investigations at each of the notable spots: the Swamp, the Money Pit, Shaft 10X, and Smith's Cove (also known as Sheerdam Cove).

First up was the Swamp, rumored to have been man-made—joining two smaller islands. Wood belonging to old Spanish sailing craft has been found within its muddy depths, along with other various out-of-place artifacts. I had been on the island for hours now, yet this was the first time I'd be actively investigating it with equipment on camera. It had been over five years since a camera crew shadowed me on the case, but I fell right back into the rhythm. I gave them the bits they needed: the perplexed look, the single eyebrow raise, and the shocked look at my recorder. Those came naturally to me as it was my default behavior on any case, but I also knew it would help the editors back in the office. Since I didn't know if I would capture any evidence during this brief sweep, I would at least give them the building blocks of an interesting edit.

I heard a buzzing nearby. A shadow passed along the ground near me, revealing the position of a drone flying overhead. All eyes were on me, and the pressure to deliver was palpable. But you should know by now that fakery is not my way, so I decided to focus on enlightening Matty with the methods of a proper investigation. I switched into training mode. Showing him my Mel Meter and explaining its use in the field, I also hoped to train the viewers who would be watching. Professor Brian had shown up, and class was in session!

Speaking of sessions, after doing a basic baseline, I took out a couple of recorders to conduct the first EVP session of the day. Matty said, if so inclined, we could wade further into the swamp. As it was, we were standing on its border atop a walkway of unconnected wooden planks. To go in deeper would mean to leave the safety of the boards and immerse ourselves in the muck. It was never mentioned on the show, but the swamp reeked! If I were to fall in, I'd never get that smell off me. Had I been booked to spend a week or more there, I might have entertained going further into the swamp, but the producers had me on an early flight the next morning, and the last thing I wanted to do was return to civilization smelling like the Bog of Eternal Stench. That was a hard pass—we could collect EVPs just as well from the edge!

The initial questions were introductory as always, but Matty wanted to cut to the chase. "Is there a ship buried in the swamp?" he inquired. The cameras continued to roll as we stood silently, waiting for a response.

The next stop on our tour was Shaft 10X, which Matty described as having the "heaviest traffic in terms of paranormal, unexplained activity." Several people had experienced sightings of a black mass moving about that area, perhaps connected to an alleged death down the shaft. The clearing around it was littered with all manner of junk. Piles of wooden slats and metal pipes were strewn around several rusty barrels. An old supply shed leaned precariously off its base as if it had fallen and could not get up. This spot felt like a Lego set not yet assembled, with its pieces spread all over the side of the hill. The trees surrounding it stood sentinel, cradling the area in their charge.

We continued to take readings and see what we felt. Another EVP session produced questions such as "What's your name?" and "Can you make a noise, so we know that it's you?" Some of the queries were answered by birds—the first animals to appear all day. Although not backed up by my Mel Meter, both of us did feel odd out there; a certain energy was afoot. If my feelings of being watched earlier could be characterized as examinatory, this felt more like being stalked—a sense that if we dallied too long or found ourselves there after dark, we'd be in danger.

Moving on to the current Money Pit (since 10X used to be considered the prime drilling spot), we accelerated our investigation even more by jumping straight into another EVP session. Human bone fragments belonging to specimens from Europe and the Middle East were discovered down the shaft. Matty wanted clarification on those particular finds.

"Are you the person whose remains we found of Middle Eastern descent?" he asked as we stared down into the massive pipe. Faint taps echoed back up. Tiny ripples were barely visible in the murky water below.

"Do you have any messages for anyone?" I added. We paused as if expecting an audible answer, then continued.

"What do you want us to do," he began, and then a loud BANG from below! Something had hit hard into the pipe, making Matty jump back and startling some crew members. Would that have happened regardless of our presence, or could it be considered a response? This was a moment that made it onto the show and was even used as one of the preview hooks. Thankfully, I kept my cool. I stood my ground and barely reacted to the loud noise. What did I tell you, Oak Island? I'm here to do a job . . .

Matty seemed genuinely surprised. "That scared the blank out of me, oh my god, that sounded like it came from down there," he said as he looked at me, then to the pit, then back to me. After spending so much time working with the Lagina brothers, who I would later find out were stout skeptics when it came to the paranormal, Matty had finally shared an experience with someone on the other side of the belief spectrum. The irony was not lost on me.

"Matty, you've been officially initiated into the world of paranormal investigating. You have arrived!" I said as I shook his hand.

Things were rolling along pretty well—each place we went seemed to offer up something different. I couldn't wait to review the audio and see if we'd captured even more than we realized. But there was one more stop to make, and the sun was getting low in the sky. We had to hurry.

Smith's Cove, on the eastern end of the island, featured a massive wall erected to keep the water back from yet another dig site. Other man-made workings had been discovered here as well, including wooden beams that appeared to have specific markings carved into them. Their purpose was still unknown. Heavy rainfall the day before had caused a massive mudslide, blanketing nearly the entire area in what looked like chocolate pudding. We found ourselves proceeding carefully, choosing how deep we wanted to go into the mud with each step. Finally making it onto a concrete landing, we composed ourselves and got ready to shoot again. The cameramen, sound guy, and producers also found suitable safe spots.

Since this area may have been a landing spot for whoever had hidden the treasure, we took a different spin with the questions. We asked if there was anyone there belonging to the Order of Solomon's Temple, better known as the Knights Templar. We empathized with how long their journey must have been and assured them that whatever they had hidden was still safe. Matty and I then started firing off questions.

"Is something of religious importance here on the island?"

"Could we be harmed if we find the treasure?"

"Is it the Ark of the Covenant?"

"Are the current searchers getting close to solving the mystery?"

"Is the seventh person on the island now?"

"When will this mystery be solved?"

We asked several more questions as well, but unfortunately, this scene did not make the cut. By the time we were done, the sun had set. It was time to return to the production village and review my evidence. I was given some time alone in the Oak Island Research Center to pore through the collected audio files. I sat down and took a deep breath, my equipment placed around me on the table with purpose.

For a moment, I was once again confronted with the nagging insecurity that had been in the back of my mind since I'd left home for the airport. What if I didn't capture anything on audio? They'd think they got the wrong guy and flew me out for nothing. It was a rushed investigation on a very short timeline, with onlookers that may have acted as blockers to potential activity—the pressure was immense! Looking out the window, I could see the crew bustling about, each tending to their jobs. I, too, had a job and put on my headphones to begin.

For each EVP session, we had two recorders going. The first, my trusty Olympus VN-7200; the second, a Zoom H4n Handy Recorder. The Olympus was my primary, and if I found anything on it,

I would check the other to verify. This was an important gig; I wanted to be thorough and do my best to deliver results. I hit play and listened carefully.

Our voices reached out to the ether, and the background tone replied in its own voice of near silence. Question after question, all I heard was the wind. My hopes were beginning to dwindle. I started to feel antsy in my seat. My sweater suddenly felt itchy. But then, just as I thought all was for naught, I heard it.

From the file recorded at the Swamp, Matty asked, "If you want us to stop searching for treasure on Oak Island, tell us to stop now." A few more seconds elapsed, and then the whispered response, "You don't trust us." That first file was only three minutes and fifty-one seconds long, and the unknown voice appeared at the 3:44 mark! Shortly after, I announced we'd be ending the session—the EVP had made it in just under the wire!

Feeling a sudden elation that banished all doubts, I stood up, threw my hands in the air, and exclaimed, "WE GOT ONE!" like Janine Melnitz in *Ghostbusters*. Though no one outside had heard me, I was now re-energized and excited to check the rest of the audio.

Listening carefully to the 10X file delivered another EVP—one that actually made it onto the episode. Matty asked, "What's your name?" Several seconds passed, and just before I spoke again with the follow-up, "Do you know who Marty is?" a voice said something that sounded like, "Chain them." In the episode, this made a certain sense because we'd been talking about a rumor concerning someone who may have died after being chained up in the shaft. But, upon further review and listening to what viewers of the episode have shared with me, I think we may have misinterpreted it. It might have been more of a direct answer than we thought. The cadence of the voice was quick, and the two words "chain them" may have been influenced by our thoughts at the time. Now, I hear it say, "Jason."

"Chain them" and "Jason" have similar phonetic sounds when spoken rapidly. I checked the list of those who died on Oak Island, hoping to find a Jason on it, but no such luck.

This is the EVP that Matty brought to Rick and Marty Lagina to represent our investigation. I could tell, as they sat there at the table with their arms crossed, that the brothers had serious doubts about the value and validity of what they were hearing, what we were claiming to have captured. I guess I can't begrudge them their skepticism—I was once where they are. It certainly explains why they didn't seem interested in meeting me during filming. They were mere feet away, and Matty said he'd introduce me, but they made themselves scarce. I chose not to take it personally. The island judged me worthy, and that victory was all I needed. I didn't even think that was the best EVP we captured.

At the Money Pit, right after that loud bang, Matty jumped and said, "What the fuck was that!" Right on the heels of that, I asked, "What do you know about the curse?" Barely a second passed before a disembodied voice said, "Thank you." Who they were thanking and why remains a mystery.

Each file I listened to delivered more evidence that I could present to the crew. I was so giddy that I wanted to call them all in to listen immediately. But I had one more to go, and I had high hopes for the Smith's Cove session. With its weighty questions, I wondered what kind of answers awaited, for at this point, I was confident there would be some! As it turned out, there was only one, to which I had a personal stake.

"Is the seventh person on the island now?" I asked.

I had quipped to several producers that I hoped they hadn't invited me out to be the seventh sacrificial death. Their responses alternated from nervous laughter to feigned amusement. I'm sure they'd heard that joke from every visitor received on the island. It was nice of them to suffer it one more time for me. The EVP response, however, was swift and decisive.

"Nooo . . ." it whispered.

Hearing it made me smile. Not only was I safe from making history posthumously, but I seemingly just confirmed that Matty and the rest of the crew were off the hook as well. Also, I was sure I'd get a response on this file, and lo and behold, I had. This was a rarity—both the number of EVPs as well as my confidence regarding them. People investigate haunted places and come away with EVPs all the time, but for me, a ratio of 1:1 was rare. Every recording had multiple hits with one clear anomaly each. It was as if the EVP gods heard my prayers when I first stepped onto the island. What made this venture so successful for me?

I've thought about it a lot and come up with the following explanation. First, I approached the island with confidence. Despite a few moments of doubt, I realized I'd been tapped for this project because of who I was and what I had achieved in the paranormal. I had a reliable reputation that took me years to cultivate. In short, I'd earned this. Second, the weather had an effect as well. I don't mean that certain light and barometric pressure levels affected the concentration of PK (a fictional unit of measurement denoting psychokinetic energy) or any other such nonsense explanation that one might hear on TV. I'm talking about its effect on me. My mood. It was a beautiful day; the sun was shining, and the air was warm, making it easy to be cheerful. I was happy to be there. Perhaps that elevated mood raised my vibration enough on a spiritual level to allow for better results. Conversely, it's known that on any investigation, if you're feeling ill or tired, it's probably best to sit it out as you'd put yourself in potential danger of attachment or worse. I'd focused on that half of the equation for years, but I hadn't considered the reverse. Like most other lessons I'd learned, it took an experience out in the world for me to truly accept the words I had often spoken to others.

***

My time on Oak Island was brief but enlightening. All who walk on it seem to take a piece of it with them while simultaneously leaving part of themselves behind. Is that the real curse? Or perhaps, it's a blessing in disguise. Becoming intertwined with the island and its story has had a positive effect on me. Today, I field more questions about my time there than I do about the entire run of *Haunted Collector*. Just as my name comes up from time to time in association with the Bermuda Triangle, now it also does so with Oak Island. So much so that I was invited to discuss the island on a recent episode of *The UnXplained* with William Shatner.

With a little positivity and confidence, I'd love to earn more such adventures. When I see advertisements on TV for *The Curse of Oak Island*, I don't think of the deaths and the desperation. Thinking of the island now brings one word to mind: hope.

22

I Can't Go for That

I shall say this up-front: this chapter has absolutely nothing to do with ghosts. Bigfoot will not make an appearance, nor will there be any sightings of spacecraft from worlds beyond. I can't even say there is a lesson associated with it.

In a few hours, I will find myself seated in one of the nosebleed sections within Madison Square Garden to see one of my favorite music acts, Daryl Hall & John Oates. As I was mentally indexing all the times I've seen them live, it occurred to me that one of my old "Big Stories" surrounded a Hall & Oates concert. Why do I include it in this collection of paranormal tales? I'm going to let you be the judge. But first, a background nugget.

The possible existence of extrasensory perception (ESP) is a main area of study in parapsychology. The ability to glean information from a source outside the five senses has been proclaimed for as long as man has walked upright, yet it's still not fully understood or even widely accepted. Precognition, telepathy, and clairvoyance are but a few of the terms associated with the research undertaken by the parapsychologist. Because the reports are difficult to prove and even harder to replicate, parapsychologists find themselves on the fringe of academia and the scientific community in what is generally considered a pseudoscience.

As the years have passed, this area of The Work is the one I've identified with most. To be clear, parapsychology and ghost hunting are not synonymous terms, but there is indeed an overlap. If spirit is in some way involved, that may explain many of the phenomena witnessed. The basics of parapsychology do not concern proving the survival of the soul but in determining the authenticity of the occurrences reported and then attempting to figure out how they work.

How many times do you analyze the origins of things that occur during the day? The frequency is probably quite low—until something happens that seems truly baffling. Looking into the sources always causes me to consider those Big Picture concepts such as predestination and a grand plan. As I've mentioned, I don't like feeling as if I have no control over my own life.

Fate plays the long game, and much of the machinations it uses can't be observed until one reflects on things that seemed inconsequential at the time. Does this mean I am a believer in it? I don't know. Let's get back to the tale at hand. Time to rewind to my teenage years.

***

Despite being unable to find a friend who wanted to accompany me to the concert, I was excited to be driving down to the Garden State Arts Center that evening with my neighbor's daughter seated next to me. We were childhood playmates because our parents were friends and lived in the same apartment building. That connection continued as both families moved into houses on the same block, but our easy friendship faded as the years passed. We each went to different schools, and during that phase of our development, a popular girl from a public school and an introverted boy from a private school had little in common anymore. Essentially, I was riding with a stranger, but given the destination, that didn't bother me in the least. I was going to see Hall & Oates in concert!

Our parents had arranged our pairing for the evening. Another pairing that facilitated the trip was how I obtained the tickets. Working as a waitress in a popular restaurant, my mother had cause to meet and develop friendships with customers that came by frequently. One such customer was the mother of a session guitarist who happened to be touring at the time with my favorite musical duo. During the many maternal conversations that transpired between them, the connection was made that their sons had one very common interest.

So it came to pass that I was given tickets to see Daryl Hall & John Oates when their tour came near later that month. I was thrilled beyond words! The only problem was that none of my friends were really into them. I had an extra ticket, and at the time, going solo was not an option I would consider. But that problem was solved with a phone call to my neighbor, whose daughter liked all kinds of music. When my mother informed me of what she did, I don't think it quite registered—I was still ecstatic about seeing the show, and that's all I could focus on.

The tickets included dinner beforehand at the venue's restaurant. As we sat and awaited our food, I thumbed through the items of the envelope I'd been given at the will-call booth. Inside were the pair of tickets, the vouchers for the pre-show meal, a couple of ad-type flyers, and a pair of hefty stickers bearing the picture of the headline act and the date. I stared at the items for a moment, categorizing them all in my mind.

"What songs do they sing again that I'd know?" she asked.

Surprised, I looked up and stared at her in disbelief. I had to remember that this was not a fellow fan but a pity date of sorts. "You Make My Dreams, Maneater, Kiss On My List—plenty of others. You'll know them when you hear them."

Today, I can wax intellectual about the full catalog of H&O songs and spout trivia about each one, but enthusiasm about anything wasn't considered cool back then. So I cut myself off there. Luckily, that's when the salads arrived. Pushing the envelope to the side, I unwrapped the heavy napkin containing the utensils and draped it across my lap. This was a proper occasion in my mind, and I wanted to behave accordingly.

Looking around the room, I saw older couples dressed nicely, conversing and enjoying their meals. Smiles and laughter abounded. At my table, however, I struggled to think of something clever to say. I was currently a junior in a Catholic all-boys high school. The ability to converse naturally with the opposite sex would not develop until sometime later. My likely awkwardness blurred most of the particulars from my memory, but I do remember the way her dark hair framed her face, her eyes bright like spotlights, causing me to inwardly shrink from their gaze. She looked comfortable in a blue tank top and was obviously used to handling social situations with ease. I assume I tried to make some funny comments, which I also assume didn't land since I can't recall what they were. It was like my own personal *Wonder Years* episode. If I listened hard enough, perhaps I'd hear Daniel Stern narrating above the meal. But she was not my

Winnie Cooper, so all I had to do was relax and be a less-nerdy version of myself. Daryl and John awaited.

Speaking of whom . . . I turned once again to the envelope and pulled out the stickers. The image of the duo was black and white, surrounded by a yellow background. The words "World Tour 1991" were printed in large letters beneath the picture, and even larger was "GUEST" stamped below that. The hair on the back of my neck stood up as I realized what I was holding. It was a difficult identification because I had never held any before (or since), but there I was with a pair of backstage passes in my hand.

"Oh my," I began, "I think these are backstage passes!" I held them up to show my companion as she buttered her dinner roll.

"You think?" she countered. She, too, was inexperienced in the currency of concert life.

"It has to be—look, there's even initials down at the bottom as if someone had to approve them," I explained.

She looked back at me with an air of skepticism. "They're probably just nice, yellow stickers," she offered.

Really? Would they do such a thing? Did these nice, yellow stickers have no other value than to simply commemorate our time at the show? My instincts were screaming at me to take them to a venue official or attempt infiltration of the backstage area with them. Still, as I'd inferred, I was not the most confident person at the time, especially when an opposing opinion was placed against my own. She didn't even seem interested in trying to find out more about them. The final nail in that coffin was her shrugging it off. This might not seem like a devastating response but remember the time. To a boy unaccustomed to being around girls, one slightly older than he, making a motion which would accentuate her burgeoning form, was everything. And in a low-cut tank top, no less. I was powerless to further the debate. Game, set, match.

Later, we would settle into our seats with said stickers and enjoy the concert. Little else of note came out of that evening. The full realization of what I'd missed came the next day when my mother got to work.

"So, how did Brian like meeting the boys?" my mother's customer inquired as coffee was poured into a waiting mug.

At this point in the Netflix series of my life, the scene cuts to my face as my mother relayed what she'd found out at work. The baseline from "I Can't Go For That (No Can Do)" begins to play as my utter shock mixed with regret fills the screen. It cuts to black, and the episode credits begin. "I'll do anything that you want me to, yeah, I'll do almost anything that you want me to, but I can't go for that. No can do."

The angst this tale would cause me grew as the years went by, and I related it to friends and colleagues. I didn't have cause to see that girl many more times as life took us on our separate paths, but any time I did, all I could think of were "nice, yellow stickers." I guess as far as mishaps went, this was definitely a First World Problem. Did I have the right to complain? Regardless, complain I did until Fate finally got the memo.

***

I closed my eyes and focused on my breathing as I sat there in the toilet stall. Dressed in a suit and tie, I tugged at my collar, which always seemed to be intent on strangling the breath out of me. Uncomfortable as it was, I looked forward to this five-minute portion of the day. I didn't need to use the facilities, but it was the only place I could hide and be alone at my new, high-pressure job.

Fresh out of college, I found myself working for a technical recruiting agency, where I had to deceptively charm my way past the systems that companies have in place to block sales calls. Secretaries, assistant managers, and automated recordings were my adversaries as my mission was to reach managers who had the power to approve hiring talent in our stables. More confrontation and rejection—oh, joy!

Making my job even more intimidating was the fact that my supervisor sat directly across from me, our tables connected with no divide or cubicle wall to offer any privacy. He would simultaneously do his work and stare at me, unblinking, the entire day. The five o'clock hour, when the madness of the evening commute overtook most of Manhattan, was my only other period of relief.

The flushing of a neighboring stall snapped me out of my comatose state. As I heard the tell-tale sounds of hands being washed, I composed myself to return to my desk and count the hours until I was free again.

Work dragged on as it always did. When I finally got to step outside, the cool September air greeted me and pulled me out of the general malaise that characterized my day. A river of men and women in professional garb rushed by, heading for the subways and bus stops. Normally, I would join that race of suits and skirts, doing my best to look important and accomplished despite feeling quite the opposite. This day was different, though. I suddenly had the desire to wander. Instead of fighting my way through the crowds heading south towards the ferry and home, I began to walk north.

With no destination in mind, I let autopilot take over. I navigated each corner with no thought or deliberation, and every step I took seemed to ease the burdens my day had placed upon me. Even the lions guarding the entrance to the New York Public Library seemed to approve of my impromptu walkabout.

Without knowing how I arrived there, I eventually found myself sitting on the "A" Train headed uptown. A man possessed I was, and soon found myself exiting to the surface. Unsure of what to do in this new neighborhood, I pondered getting something to eat. Those thoughts were pushed back when I saw what stood across the street from the station—an HMV record store. I find it strange to think that there might be readers who have never heard of it or don't know what a record store is, but in 1997, it was still in existence—

although the change in the music industry had already begun its decline.

MTV was showing fewer and fewer music videos. The musical acts I grew up with were getting older and not releasing albums as often, and when they did, one had to search for the details. I can recall one of those mornings leaving late for work because I had a hunch that the video for "Congo," Genesis's new single from their latest album, would air. I absolutely had to see it before work, or they might never play it again. Were the chiding remarks I got from my supervisor worth the effort? Yes. I did see the video that morning, and I never saw it on television again. Genesis would end their recording days shortly after that.

Back then, this was my world—one full of change, and I wasn't handling it well. I was a zombie trapped in a machine of repetition, with no idea if it would get better or worse. I needed a sign.

Crossing the street and going into the store, my mood was immediately lifted. The décor was bright and inviting, with shelves and rows that meandered in winding patterns, offering an adventure of discovery for the music aficionado. A blazing guitar riff played out over the department speakers, the start of a song I'd never heard before. Driving notes followed, taking over my body, making my head bop and my shoulders sway.

Moments later, I was startled by a tap on the shoulder, interrupting my solo dance party. Turning around, I encountered a middle-aged man wearing a casual suit with a "STAFF" sticker affixed to his lapel. Were my moves so bad that security had to be dispatched to stop me?

"Excuse me, are you a Hall and Oates fan?" he asked.

What a random yet specific question—I was momentarily confused, and it took me a second to find my words. "Yeah," I managed to croak out.

"Great, do you want to meet the guys?" he continued.

Pause.

What exactly was going on here? Was someone playing a trick on me? The show, *Punk'd* would not exist for another six years, and I don't think anyone thought they'd end up on *Candid Camera* anymore. But who did he mean—he couldn't possibly be talking about who I thought he was talking about, could he?

The music from overhead pushed its way into my main focus. I didn't know the song, but I knew the voice—it was Daryl Hall.

Looking past the man facing me, I noticed a poster on the wall. It was yellow, and at its center was the image of Daryl and John walking on a beach with the words "NEW ALBUM BY DARYL HALL & JOHN OATES: MARIGOLD SKY—IN STORE APPEARANCE TODAY." As I read those words, I became aware that the man was still talking to me. ". . . to promote the new album," he finished.

The pieces fell into place quickly. I nodded in the affirmative and followed him towards the back of the store. I felt slightly numb; it was all happening so fast. I only had a few moments to process what was about to happen when I found myself in a back room on a very short line. On the other end, mere feet away was the duo from Philly themselves!

The line had a wide demographic of people. I was probably the youngest but arguably the most excited. Time flew by in a whirlwind as I made it to the front, met them both, and shook their hands. I think someone took a picture, but before everyone had a smartphone, there was no way for me to obtain a copy. I was then ushered back out to a small stage area where I was instructed to stand in the front. The small group of people who also participated in the meet and greet was up there with me. Shortly, they would perform.

I couldn't believe my luck! I had just met Hall and Oates. I was now inches away from the stage they were about to perform on. The setlist was taped to the floor, all the instruments were in place, and across the store, speakers announced that in five minutes, a special set would begin!

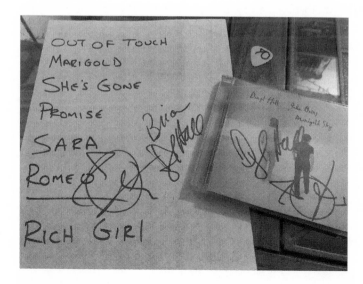

The performance was incredible. My finding it felt magical. I beamed all the way home with an autographed CD, John Oates's guitar pick, and the setlist in my possession. My Hall and Oates tale had a new, happy ending. Because of this, I didn't spend much time pondering the whys of the event. I was just satisfied to have gotten cosmic reparations.

***

But here I am years later, looking back, and now I do have questions. How did this come to be? I had no prior knowledge of the album coming out. Hence, I had no idea they would be doing in-store appearances to support it. Did my previous experience and subsequent dwelling on it put in a ticket to the Universe saying I was due a windfall? That's not exactly the Law of Attraction, nor is it Karma. The mishap with my neighbor's daughter wasn't done on purpose. There was no malice involved; it was just one of those things. So what made me skip going home and wander the city after work? In a city of over seven million people, what had led me straight to the spot where one of my favorite musical acts was going to be performing? Could it have been a form of extrasensory perception?

Put yourself in the place of a parapsychologist hearing this tale. Could this all be ascribed to simple luck, or is there something greater behind it? Upon hearing the particulars of the story, it is the task of that parapsychologist to decide whether or not it is authentic and worthy of further study. Being that this kind of occurrence only happened to me one time (that I am aware of), I would say that such a researcher would not look deeper. But still, I wonder. If it wasn't a function of my mental ability, then was it part of that Grand Plan I continue to rage against? If so, it's evident there are good moments written in the book of my life. Surprise moments that will bring me joy with no preparation involved.

For all the hardships and pain I may endure, there will be elation, too. This is the part I have always struggled with. If I am in control of my destiny, then I wonder why sometimes things work out and sometimes they don't. Why doesn't hard work always translate into reward? If I believe, let go, and allow Fate to guide my life, then I'm left questioning the timing of things. It's impotence that frustrates the enlightened.

Some believe in reincarnation. Those who do also believe that we choose who we come back as, including the milestones visited along the way. The theory is that each pass through this life teaches us a lesson that will bring us closer to our highest vibration, at which point we no longer have to come back. Again, more faith. Now, if that is so, then perhaps both states are true—there is a plan, *and* we have free will, but that free will is exercised before our birth.

Knowing the details of the road already traveled gives us the insight to choose the next leg of the journey. So the vehicle is then selected, the options assigned, and the price set.

I've spoken about balance before, but this model preempts the need for it, since that balance might exist across the entire continuum, thereby making it impossible for us to measure. It's a huge concept to digest. It's simple to state but difficult to truly grasp. It comes down to vantage point—we're too close to it. It's like the Nazca lines in Peru. These huge geoglyphs form various shapes, from simple geometric ones to complex depictions of animals such as a monkey, spider, jaguar, and more. While standing on the ground, if the lines are even detectable, it is nearly impossible to see the whole image. But from above, on the mountains and especially in the air, the pictures spring to life. Perhaps our life paths are like those lines, and while we're Earthbound, the proverbial Big Picture cannot be viewed in whole.

So, did I choose this priceless experience with Daryl and John? What shape did I carve into the ground for myself—Oates's mustache? What is the lesson here? Perhaps it is patience. I've never been good with that virtue. As a species, we know we have so little time here that it can be hard to consciously slow down and allow things to happen.

I'm still unsure if this tale can be considered evidence of supernatural ability or a universal blueprint. But it has taught me that to move forward, we sometimes have to look back. Even if not part of a divine greater plan, all the stories of my past can help guide my next steps. Now that, I can go for.

Epilogue

I'd wanted to write (and complete) a book for close to thirty years without doing anything about it. I wrote the first draft of this book in just under five months, although it felt much longer as each chapter had me revisiting past adventures in my life. Now, here I am, writing the conclusion, the final part, tying the bow on the present I now give away. The sense of completion, the elation of having completed a task that I once thought insurmountable, feels incredible.

To me, it's like reaching the end credits of *Forrest Gump* or *The Curious Case of Benjamin Button*. Both take the viewer on time-spanning journeys, and when they close, you feel as if you've lived life along with the main characters. After walking with me on this beach of existential tales, I hope you feel likewise.

Each anecdote—each grain of sand—provides a personal glimpse into some of the most poignant moments in my journey thus far, and in sharing them with you, I found myself analyzing again what each one meant for me in a Big Picture way. What did I learn, and how did I grow? I trust similar questions were on your mind and that my experiential lessons, my still unanswered questions, have somehow moved you further along in your life journey.

In the chapter Hooked On a Feeling, I joked about being the one who did all the listening and that maybe I should have my own practice. But in these pages, it was you, the reader, listening to me, and for that, I am grateful.

Remember, I started my paranormal career as a skeptic, but I've evolved and changed over the years, and each of my experiences was a step in that evolution. Be it getting touched inappropriately in a prison, accepting the nature of empathy, or understanding the balance of the Universe; I had to come to terms with each lesson in my own time. Each of you will do the same, in your own time, along your own paths.

As I often say on *Paranormal Caught On Camera*: spirits just want to tell their stories.

I've been lucky enough to tell mine before shuffling off that mortal coil.

About the Author

Brian J. Cano is not only a recognized expert in the paranormal community, he is also a pioneer of the paranormal television movement. His cable access show Scared on Staten Island (later titled SCARED!) garnered significant regional popularity and became an influential predecessor to similar shows on major networks. From there, Brian's platform continued to grow as a fixture at conventions and events across the country. His scientific and reasoned approach to paranormal investigating, along with his technical expertise, landed him on Syfy's Haunted Collector with John Zaffis. Brian has also appeared on History Channel's The Curse of Oak Island and The UnXplained hosted by William Shatner, TRVL Channel's Most Terrifying Places in America, and he is currently a featured analyst for TRVL's Paranormal Caught on Camera, now in its fifth season.

With decades of experience, Brian stands apart in this growing field for his passion to educate others, not just entertain them; to open their minds to the reality of paranormal phenomena, but with healthy measures of skepticism and rational insight, and as a source of existential discovery. When not filming, Brian can be found sharing his wit and wisdom as a keynote speaker at major conferences and universities throughout the US and abroad. He also routinely holds events of his own at haunted hotspots. Additionally, Brian hosts international tours in a global pursuit of the paranormal, and his trailblazing History of the Paranormal exhibit is presently making its inaugural tour at unique historical locations across the US. Learn more at neverstopsearching.com.